How to Analyze People and Dark Psychology 2 manuscripts in 1

Best Strategies for Body Language. Reading People, Mind Control and Manipulation!

Written By Beto Canales & Habits of Wisdom

© **Copyright 2019 Beto Canales & Habits of Wisdom - All rights reserved.**

The content contained within this book may not be reproduced, duplicated or transmitted without direct written permission from the author or the publisher.

Under no circumstances will any blame or legal responsibility be held against the publisher, or author, for any damages, reparation, or monetary loss due to the information contained within this book. Either directly or indirectly.

Legal Notice:

This book is copyright protected. This book is only for personal use. You cannot amend, distribute, sell, use, quote or paraphrase any part, or the content within this book, without the consent of the author or publisher.

Disclaimer Notice:

Please note the information contained within this document is for educational and entertainment purposes only. All effort has been executed to present accurate, up to date, and reliable, complete information. No warranties of any kind are declared or implied. Readers acknowledge that the author is not engaging in the rendering of legal, financial, medical or professional advice. The content within this book has been derived from various sources. Please consult a licensed professional before attempting any techniques outlined in this book.

By reading this document, the reader agrees that under no circumstances is the author responsible for any losses, direct or indirect, which are incurred as a result of the use of information contained within this document, including, but not limited to, — errors, omissions, or inaccuracies.

How to Analyze People and Dark Psychology 2 manuscripts in 1

Table of Contents

Book - I

Introduction 9

    Pay Close Attention to Nonverbal Cues 11

    Concentrate on Your Tone When Speaking 12

    Maintain Eye Contact 13

Chapter 1: The Psychology Behind Reading Body Language 14

    What is Body Language? 15

    The Importance of Body Language 16

    Origin of Humans and Body Language 17

    How to Read Body Language 18

Chapter 2: The Significance of Learning and Understanding Non-verbal Communication 29

    Factors Affecting Understanding of Body Language ...31

Chapter 3: Principles of Body Language 35

Chapter 4 : Basic Tips on Body Language 38

    How to Read People's Body Language 41

Chapter 5: The Language Differences in Sexes 52

    Men's Body Language 53

    Female Body Language 59

Chapter 6: Benefits of Knowing How to Read Body Language and Facial Expressions 66

Enhance Parenting Skills 66

  Give Good Impression in Job Interviews 67

  Nourish Personal Relationships 68

  Identify and Read Negative Nonverbal Behavior 68

  Project Yourself Positively 70

  Facial Profiling 72

  Hair 75

  Eyebrows 77

  Eyes 81

  Nose 84

  Cheeks 85

  Lips 86

  Identifying Personality Types 90

Chapter 7: Learning, Recognizing, and Reading Hidden Body Messages 121

  Knowing When Someone is Lying 123

  Reading People on a Date 126

  Communicating Effectively in an Interview 128

  Reading Power Cues 131

Chapter 8: Knowledge and Techniques Required to Understand and Interpret Body Language 134

  How Body Language is Connected to Emotional Quotient (EQ) 134

  Ways to Gauge EQ Through Body Language 139

Chapter 9: Reading and Understanding Different Cues 144

Emotional Cues 150
Attraction Cues 152
Relational Cues 155

Chapter 10: Understanding Non-Verbal Cues for Success in Career and Business 158

Microexpressions to be Aware of When Negotiating . 158
Reading Body Language to Win Negotiations 162
Body Signals to Look for in a Negotiation 163
Signs that You Have the Other Person's Full Attention 170
Tell-Tale Signs of Disagreement 171

Chapter 11: Is Faking Body Language Possible? 173

Microexpressions 173

Chapter 12: Training Exercises to Improve Body Language 178

Body Language Exercises (Solo) 178
Body Language Exercises (Group Activity) 183

Conclusion 198

Book - II

Introduction 200

Chapter 1: What is Dark Psychology 204

Chapter 2: Are You at Risk for Manipulation 221

Chapter 3: Expressions that Carry Weight 239

Chapter 4 : What Makes People Tick 264

Chapter 5 : Techniques of Dark Psychology You Might Not Be Aware Of 279

Chapter 6 : Nasty Tricks 299

Chapter 7 : Damaged by Dark Psychology 318

Chapter 8 : Reading People, the Right Way 338

Chapter 9 : Kickstart to Analyzing People 357

Summary 391

Book - I

How to Analyze People

Instantly Learn Body Language, Social Skills, and Secret Techniques that Psychologists and FBI Agents Use to Read People

Introduction

Have you ever wanted to know when people are telling lies or know the real intention of a romantic interest? It can be quite depressing to not get a deal because you didn't know what went through your client's head.

Almost everyone has experienced some dilemma in one way or another because their instincts weren't strong when needed or simply because they didn't listen to their gut and did otherwise.

This isn't about your gut or instinct, but one thing is for sure. You want the ability to READ PEOPLE LIKE A BOOK!

This sounds incredibly impossible but NOT ANYMORE! Read this book and you'll find out how amazing it is to read someone, detect lies, and learn more about your romantic interests.

How would you want to perfectly close a deal simply by guessing a client's next reactions and knowing what tickles him?

Body language refers to nonverbal signals we use when we are communicating with other people. These nonverbal signals make up a large part of our daily communications.

Though we are thinking that we effectively convey our message using words, it could be surprising to learn that our body movements and facial expressions - things we don't actually say can convey more volumes of information than those we convey through words.

Let's take this for an illustration. A frown can indicate sadness or disapproval while a smile is a sign that the person is happy or approves of whatever it is that is being presented. In most cases, our facial expressions reveal our inner feeling while in a particular situation. However, verbal and nonverbal communication can sometimes be contradicting. In this case, it is more useful if you know how to decipher the person's nonverbal cues and signals than merely rely on their words. This can be especially true when you are negotiating for a deal, dealing with a cheating partner, or taking a crucial job interview.

There are also times when you can get away from a lurking danger because you can read danger cues of charming strangers or save yourself from embarrassment because you were able to reverse the situation even before others recognize it.

An expression on a person's face can help us determine if we can trust or believe what they are saying. There is one study that revealed that the most trustworthy facial expression bears a slight smile with a slight raise of the eyebrows.

By learning the skill of reading body language and micro expressions, you will be able to:

- Understand the meaning behind a person's body language
- Read people's thoughts before they even speak out
- Analyze personality through body language cues
- Know when your partner is cheating on you
- Detect when someone is telling a lie
- Identify positive and negative body signals

Learning a strong communication skill can help you in both your personal and professional life. While verbal communication is important, it constitutes less than 50% of your daily interpersonal communication.

So, how can you improve your nonverbal communication?

Pay Close Attention to Nonverbal Cues

People communicate information in a number of ways. You need, therefore, to pay attention to the following:

- Eye contact
- Body movements

- Posture
- Gestures
- Tone of voice

All of these signals convey important data that aren't put into words. By paying attention to these unspoken behaviors, you can likewise improve your own ability to communicate nonverbally.

Spot Incongruent Behaviors

If a person displays nonverbal behaviors that don't match their words, pay extra attention. Would you believe someone telling you they're happy when a frown cuts deep across their face?

When someone says something that greatly contradicts their body language, it's useful to pay close attention to these subtle cues.

Concentrate on Your Tone When Speaking

Your own tone of voice carries a myriad of information especially of emotions on varied intensities. Notice you others respond to your tone of voice and try to use it in emphasizing ideas to want to communicate across.

If you are trying to show genuine interest on what someone is telling you, you can express your enthusiasm with an animated tone of voice. This will not only convey your own feelings about what is being relayed but likewise generate interest in people listening to you.

Maintain Eye Contact

Good eye contact is another significant nonverbal communication skill you need to develop. Without eye contact, the person you are talking to may feel you're uncomfortable with them or hiding something which can emit a negative feeling. On the other hand, using too much of this, you can appear to be intimidating or confrontational.

While you need to use eye contact in communicating, it is also important to learn that good eye contact is not necessarily fixing your stares on someone's eye.

Learning how to read body language will tell you all the difference between negative and positive body movements, expressions, and gestures and how they affect other people as well.

Chapter 1: The Psychology Behind Reading Body Language

We always hear people say action speaks louder than words - the impact even of a passive action is sure to hit you more than words can say.

Words unspoken are subtly exhibited through body language and some studies suggest that it constitutes more than 60 percent of what a person is trying to communicate. Learning to read and analyze unspoken words through nonverbal cues is, therefore, a skill that is valuable and beneficial. It carries a myriad of benefits. It could help you avoid possible danger or it could help someone else in need.

Have you ever heard of an abducted youth who was saved by law enforcement because the security guard of the condominium where her or she was kept was able to quickly read body language? Yes, reading body language and the facial expressions of a person can save a life!

How a person rolls their eyes or how facial expressions change can reveal what a person is thinking or hiding inside. Even a smile can have many variations. It can be sweet one or could be an evil smirk. You just have to be quick enough to identify expressions to know if a person's smile conveys pleasure or actually something in contrast.

However, before we go much further, let's define what body language is.

What is Body Language?

Body language is a type of nonverbal communication where physical behaviors are utilized to convey information relating to thoughts and feelings of the individual who may or may not be consciously relaying the message. Such behaviors include eye movement, body posture, gestures facial expressions, touch, or even the use of space.

Simply put, body language is the unspoken element of communication that our mind is using to reveal our real emotions. If we are conscious of our body language, we can adjust it to project a more positive personality.

When talking about body language, we consider the subtle cues we are sending and receiving nonverbally. To get started, we can break it into different channels.

Knowing how to read micro-expressions is significant in understanding nonverbal behavior. There are seven universal micro-expressions that are seen on a person's face based on the emotions being experienced. It is difficult to fake a micro-expression.

This is a term used to refer to our body movement in a certain space. Basically, it is the study of space and how we relate to it - how we are more or less comfortable in a certain space.

These refer to all extensions of our body including hairstyles, jewelry, clothes, and accessories. How we act and go about with our ornaments tells more about us. Are you constantly touching your hair? Do you love wearing strong colors or a scent? These are all body cues that tell more about your personality and behavior. They are your body language.

The Importance of Body Language

In the 1960s, Albert Mehrabian conducted a study on the significance of gestures and intonations for conveying a certain message and the result showed that 7 percent of communication is verbal or with the use of words. Thirty-eight percent is paraverbal (use of tone and intonation) but 55 percent is nonverbal!

If armed with this knowledge, no one can keep a secret from a person who knows how to read these signs. If you have this skill, you can be good at playing poker, negotiating a deal, cross-examining a suspect, or catching a cheater. You can do and use a lot more of these to your advantage. The study may disclose everything, but the point is words are not enough to convey or understand a message. However, being able to read people like an open book will really put you at an advantage in almost all situations. Seeing a person's strengths and weaknesses in plain view will always give you a head start.

Origin of Humans and Body Language

The origin of body language goes back to the prehistoric time when men were not aware of their ability to communicate through verbal language. They only communicated via the sign language.

Some of these nonverbal signals are universal. Everyone can easily understand when someone is happy through the smile on their face. Agony is expressed when in pain - physical or emotional while a sullen expression exhibits loneliness and desolation.

But why are some expressions easily understood regardless of the differences in culture? How come body language breaks cultural communication barriers?

We have difficulty studying the evolution of language because the evidence is so sparse, and it does not leave any fossils. Only the uncovered skulls of Homo sapiens told our geologists and sociologists the overall shape and sizes of a hominid brain but not what it can do. All that was left in addition to the skull was the shape of the early man's vocal tract consisting of tongue, mouth, and throat.

It was not until the emergence of the modern humans that there were changes in the vocal tract that may have caused speech to be faster and more expressive. Some research even suggested that language began as a sign language before it gradually switched to the vocal modality.

How to Read Body Language

There are two sides to reading body language: Decoding and encoding.

Encoding is the ability to send or relay cues to others. This is the first impression that you give to other people and it is how you make them feel with you around.

Decoding is the ability to send cues to other people. It is how you read and interpret emotion, personality, and information people are trying to hide.

It's obvious that we humans are the only creatures that use words as communication. Animals, on the other hand, use nonverbal language and distinct sounds to communicate.

Whatever you do or whenever you speak, your body releases signals unknowingly. Those signals are read by others that see your body language. Most people believe it to be more reliable and more sincere than your very words. Your gestures speak a lot about your personality so that onlookers will tend to think of it as more accurate and true than what you actually say. So, it is really important that your words and actions synchronize so that you will not be at risk of delivering ambiguous messages and lose your credibility.

Do you remember a situation where you needed to use a service? People usually tell you all the things that you want to hear. They look sincere and friendly but there's something inside you that tells you not to trust them or that you don't like them; you are not at ease with them.

It could be because they haven't established a good rapport with you and without rapport, it will be difficult to work or be at ease with them. On the contrary, it could also be because their actions are incongruent with what they say or you've caught accidentally a body signal that they actually didn't mean to release. You call it most of the time a hunch or a gut reaction.

Because of these circumstances, you need to be aware of your body language signals to be an influencer and a better communicator. Then you can learn how to listen and understand other people's nonverbal language so that you can be a better communicator and have the ability to establish rapport. Anyway, every person has the natural ability to read body language for fifteen minutes and you can enhance it by teaching yourself and through practice.

Here are some points to consider when developing the skill:

Congruence

Be sure that your body language synchronizes with your words so that you won't give unintended messages.

Clear Mind

Concentrate on your goal or output. Your mind must understand clearly what you want to communicate and what your expected output is. It will not only motivate you but it will also bring out the natural genuineness in your words and gestures. Otherwise, if there is something that you don't understand clearly, it will surely reflect in your body signals even though it may not show in your words.

Believe Yourself

How could you make others believe in what you say if you don't believe it yourself? The tip here is that you believe your own words so that your body will correctly convey the message. According to the behavior cycle model, what you believe creates and affects your behavior (this includes your body language). Even if you don't believe what you are saying, tell it to yourself a couple of times so that you believe in it. Later, your body language will follow and synchronize with your words.

Avoid Exaggerations

Whenever you exaggerate by stressing out points, the more your body signals will betray you. So, if you are trying to be convincing, be brief and straight to the point.

Relax

When your muscles are tense, there is pressure building up inside. That means, natural looking body language is at risk. Just relax, take a deep breath and exhale. Your body will relax and your shoulders will drop. You can also shake your hands and feet a little to ease the tension. Just be sure that nobody sees you.

No Statues and Poker Faces

People will most likely be curious about why you are expressionless or remain as stiff as a statue. Using the poker-face technique is not a good option since it will make people wonder what you are hiding when you do so. It is good that you are conscious of what message your body will emit and when you try to control it. But move a little and act naturally. This will make people believe that you are sincere in what you say and do.

No Over-the-Top Hand Gestures

Hand gestures above the shoulders or high hand gestures will make you look awkward and less incongruent with what you are saying. This will also make you look that you are trying too hard. Just make your hand gestures between your waist and shoulders.

Avoid Fiddling and Comforting Habits

You may not be aware that you have pet fiddles. These are small, conscious or unconscious gestures that you do when you are anxious or you feel unsure. To determine if you have pet fiddles, ask a friend to observe your gestures for a while and tell you his or her observations. You can also do it yourself by recording your usual routines on a daily basis. You may discover that you fiddle with your hair, tie, jewelry, or your eyeglasses (if you wear them). If you have pet fiddles, train yourself to refrain from doing them. But if you still feel uncomfortable without fiddling, divert to something less noticeable like rubbing gently on the insides of your palm or thumb.

Trust and Honesty

If you are honest with what you say, you will have no problem with your body language. It will just be natural for you to be congruent with what you are saying especially when you trust others with what you are thinking and feeling instead of holding back. The best way to communicate is being true to yourself and avoid being sensitive and judgmental.

Feedback Mechanism and Reading Others

Gestures can have various interpretations just as a word can have a lot of definitions. But to be accurate in reading nonverbal intent, you have to consider the accompanying clues that go along with it.

Here are some basic tips:

- Arms that are crossed mean the person is either angry or anxious. It may also mean that he or she feels cold.
- Folded arms signals displeasure and the person wants to cut off what the other is saying. It could also indicate the other person feels comfortable doing it.
- Nose touching means that the person wants to cover up a lie but it can also simply mean that the nose is itchy.

Closed and Open Non-Verbal Communication

Observe a person's gestures when you negotiate with them and determine whether they have open or closed body language.

A closed body gesture means that the person you are negotiating with has a form of discomfort such as nervousness, fear, anxiety or hostility. This form of body language consists of gestures and posture that draw the body of the person in and towards the body itself. When the limbs are tense and closed in, the body appears smaller. When there is not much eye contact and the arms are folded, it often creates a barrier between the one who performs the action and the other person who sees it.

Open body language includes gestures or positions that indicate comfort, attentiveness, and relaxation. It welcomes the other person though it may also mean to others that you make yourself vulnerable to them. Otherwise, you show them that you are comfortable with them. When you exhibit open body language, your hands are in view and your palms are exposed. Good eye contact is present, and you are free and easy with your legs and posture.

Calibration

Sizing up a person's body language is a good tactic. Try to ask questions that you are guaranteed truthful answers—questions that have obvious answers—and pay attention. Do this at least three times to form a steady baseline. If you notice changes in the baseline during the conversation, something is not right.

Practice being aware of other people's body language and try to decipher their gestures and posture by paying attention and staying in tune to what they are doing—it speaks so much about the person.

Most of the time, people tend to focus on their own thinking or what they are trying to say instead of noticing the other person's nonverbal communication. They even tend to forget or ignore what others are actually saying. If you try to observe other's actions consciously or unconsciously, you can become a better communicator.

Use It to Establish Rapport

When you speak with other people face to face, do you avoid looking at them most of the time? As for the others, when they speak, do you notice that they look away, too. Whenever you choose to look away, you are trying to remember vividly the situation by visualizing the moment, reliving your emotions or maybe you are searching for the right words that will fit into your story.

Establish rapport whenever you listen attentively and at the same time, you can also enhance your skills in reading body language. Just like when we talk on the phone, we make sounds that will ensure the other person that we are speaking to is still listening. It's also the same when we listen to the person who is talking to us (in face to face dialogue) although we don't make sounds.

Those who are experienced in communicating with other people slightly lean forward to the speaker as they make eye contact. These gestures assure the other person that they have their full attention, that they are listening, and they are keen on hearing more from the speaker. But listeners do not continuously stare because it will convey that they are not genuinely interested in the speaker's message.

Feel Comfortable or Just Chill

Relax. When you make yourself comfortable with another person, that person will also feel at ease with you. So, if you want a natural and enjoyable conversation, just relax to allow communication to flow smoothly.

You must not overlook and interpret a person's intention just because you identified the meaning of a single body gesture. Remember that when other words are used to construct a sentence, a group of body gestures can accurately point out the real intention of the portrayer. Here's a sample situation:

When a person crosses their arms, it may mean that they only feel cold. But when it is accompanied with back leaning, a step, or stiffening up, it means the person disagrees with what you are saying.

So, be observant and gather clues first before you conclude.

Chapter 2: The Significance of Learning and Understanding Non-verbal Communication

Non-Verbal Communication helps people to:

Reinforce or Modify What Has Been Spoken

When a person vehemently denies something, he or she will not just say "no!" They will include vigorous head movements to show strong disagreement.

When you meet a friend and ask how he or she is, the automatic answer is "I'm fine" with an added shoulder shrug. You may also notice that the person feels uncomfortable and can't look straight at you.

Convey Information About Emotional State

The way you communicate—the tone of voice, facial expression, and body language can tell people how you feel even without you telling them. How often have you heard people say "Are you sick?" or "You don't look fine!"

We know people can tell your state of emotion by simply looking at you.

Define or Reinforce Relationships Between People

When observing couples, you may notice how their movements are reflective of each other—holding hands, smiling, gazing into each other's eyes, etc. All these gestures are reinforcing their relationships; creating a strong bond, connecting them further.

Provide Feedback to the Other Person

When listening intently, you focus your eyes on the speaker letting them know that they have your full attention. Hand gestures indicate whether you are comfortable with another person or if you want to say something. When you agree, it is often accompanied by the nodding of your head or a slight upward movement of your brows when you are in doubt.

Regulate Communication Flow

There are many nonverbal cues to signal if you want conversation or a discussion to go on. An emphatic nod can indicate that you are in complete agreement with the speaker and have nothing more to say. On the other hand, connecting with the speaker along with a slight nod of the head can also imply that you wish to say something else.

Factors Affecting Understanding of Body Language

Understanding body language means seeing more than what you can see in the physical sense.

A person with arms folded could mean many different things:

- Feeling defensive
- Acting superior
- Judging
- Feeling relaxed

Here are the five points that will help you understand and see body language and non-verbal communication in a more realistic way:

Cues

When you act, it's not a stand-alone thing. You act in response to the actions done by others. Their actions caused by other people are what we call "triggers" that stimulate inner responses in us. Hence, seeing someone perform a particular action should make you ask yourself what led you to interpret their body language.

Cues can, likewise, occur internally in the case of thoughts and concerns leading to changes in body position. You may also ask yourself this, "Given this body language, what is the person thinking or feeling?"

You must be on the lookout for changes in a person's body language such as movements in the hands or legs, which is a sign of discomfort.

Once you see changes, look to see if there are clues to what triggered such change. An example is when someone lied and is confronted with a revealing question. There is this tendency to look away or lose eye contact.

Salesmen, likewise, study a customer's facial expressions, personal space, cheerful tones, and positive responses. Understanding their customer's body language is a signal to move further to close the deal.

Clusters

While changes in body language can single an action such as the crossing of arms, they often appear as a series of movements like when a person leans back a little, folds their arms, raises their eyebrows, and purses their lips. All these actions could mean one thing - disagreement.

A cluster of changes in body language all indicate one common emotion being felt at the moment. There are times when this cluster involves contradicting movements like when a person smiles but doesn't look straight or rubs their nose to hide discomfort. This indicates lying.

Character

Another explanation would be the general character of an individual. A person who is an introvert may use concise gestures as opposed to an extrovert who may display frequent and exaggerated body movements.

If you have no knowledge of an individual's character, it could be easy to confuse these gestures with timidity and exhibitionism. In seeking ways to predict a person's actions, we often make misinterpretations because of limited body signals and thereby assess and filter what we see based on incorrect mental models. Moods, temperaments, and other short-term emotions can also cause changes in our body language making it more difficult to interpret. However, if you are able to determine an individual's current emotional state, then you can apply this information to gain a better understanding of their actions.

Context

Lastly, the final factor to keep in mind when reading body language is the larger context that has a great influence on how the individual thinks, feels, and acts.

Events that may affect an individual can have a great impact on body language like when a person suddenly shifts their gaze, turns direction, and feel uncomfortable. It could be possible that the person suddenly saw someone they want to avoid and wants to get away. If you aren't aware of the situation, you won't be able to tell sudden changes in body language.

Chapter 3: Principles of Body Language

Body language plays a major role when people perceive your personality. Take listening skills for instance. Listening skills are a body language that most professions such as public service in particular, requires good relationships with clients. If you are a good listener, people tend to feel more comfortable with you even when you offer business advice, help people maintain their personal relationships with others, or give simple advice when you counsel them for any kind of problem that they may have.

Having poor body language can be a huge disadvantage when building future business relationships. Your nonverbal language tells people if you are genuinely interested in them and will determine your relationship. Therefore, it is very important to listen attentively to every word that's spoken and show sincere interest in regard to concerns.

The list below displays habits to avoid when listening:

- The habitual crossing of arms over your chest
- Impatient toe-tapping

- Leaning away
- Turning to look away often
- No eye contact or looking everywhere while a person is speaking

If you have any of these habits, people will think that you are not interested in what they're saying and may end your business relationship.

Try the steps below to improve your overall body language:

- Look at the person squarely in the face.
- To send a positive signal, avoid looking away.
- During communication, display an open pose. Never fold your arms or legs because the person that you are talking to will think that you are not interested in listening.
- Lean forward while you are talking to someone. This means that you are paying attention.
- Maintain normal eye contact because it is crucial. Otherwise, it will show that you're not interested or comfortable.
- Maintain a relaxed posture – not too stiff or formal when you talk. Feel comfortable.

People aren't aware of how their body language speaks and communicates to others most of the time especially when they have no knowledge of its existence and importance.

Did you know that your body speaks to you all the time? You may not be conscious about it, but the moment you meet another person, your body communicates with them. Your body communicates through your hand gestures, stance, and the way you sit, even if words do not come out of your mouth. That is how other people perceive your way of communication.

But if your body language contradicts your intentions? Unfortunately, if that happens, onlookers will get the wrong message and it could damage your credibility. To prevent this from happening, you must have a clear understanding of body language.

You can maintain credibility by making a positive entrance positive every time you meet a business client. How? Talk about business as soon as you enter the room. This will ensure you are really interested, and you mean business. Searching for your briefcase and shuffling through paper will make a negative impression. If you have to wait for your customer, read a magazine.

Chapter 4 : Basic Tips on Body Language

Use the following tips to make a positive impression:

- Provide a warm and firm hand shake.
- Choose the most accessible seat and sit immediately.
- Do not give your customer the impression that you will sit only when you are asked to do so.
- Be mindful of the space between you and the customer. Never sit too far or too close.

Choose a seat according to your client's personality. If you think your client is a shy type, sit further away. The ideal distance between you and your client is between 20-50 inches. If you want to stress a certain point, lean forward to get closer.

Eye contact is essential, and it says a lot about your personality that should never go unnoticed.

If you want people to get the impression that you are honest, sincere and open, good eye contact plus a smile will do the trick. Poor eye contact and uneasy eyes (eyes that look in all directions repeatedly) mean that you lack self-confidence. Constantly staring at the another person will also make them feel uncomfortable.

Your voice also plays an important role. Your tone is actually more important than the very words that you speak. Here, your body language is the tone of your voice so try to speak in your usual tone. When you use a normal tone and normal volume range, your body language is in an excellent state. If you want to exhibit professionalism, a well-modulated voice with a normal rate and rhythm shows passion and interest. If you want to grab your listener's attention, speak passionately. On the contrary, if you needlessly clear your throat or use 'ah' or 'um', this may mean that you are feeling anxious. Also, avoid using complicated sentences.

Focus on your gestures and posture to develop your body language. The following are simple tips to improve your posture and gestures:

Walk in an open manner- your posture should be erect when you stand; take easy and determined steps while your arms are swinging.

Demonstrate genuine listening- touch the bridge of your nose with your hand, cup your chin in between your index finger and thumb as you keep eye contact.

If you want to avoid negative impressions, try to avoid bad body language. Nervous movements can indicate disinterest. Be conscious of the body language that you transmit and avoid looking anxious. The following list includes common negative habits:

These habits mean that you disagree with another person's point of view:

- Crossing your legs
- Folding your arms over your chest
- Trying to pick up imaginary lint from your clothes
- Moving your hands on and around your face

These habits indicate a negative attitude:

- Coughing several times
- Blinking repeatedly
- Looking far away while the other person is speaking
- Shifting the eyes quickly and looking in different directions

The following may indicate frustration:

- Pointing your index finger at something
- Playing with your hair
- Wringing your hands

- Firmly clenching your hands

The following may indicate boredom:

- You don't focus your eyes on the speaker or no eye contact
- You sit with sloppy body posture
- You are preoccupied on something other than the person who is speaking

However, the importance of body language is more significant when you encounter people of diverse cultures.

Understanding body language is essential but you also need to take heed of other cues like context. Generally, it helps to see these signals as a group rather than just paying attention to a single action. When you are trying to read or interpret body language, here are the things you must watch out for:

How to Read People's Body Language

There are many ways we can convey emotions or messages through facial expressions. At times, you may express love, pity, anger, sadness, etc. to your partner through facial expressions. On the other hand, your partner must try to guess what emotion you are trying to convey. If you are good at reading emotions, then you can easily guess as long as your partner is good at conveying the emotion he or she was asked to project.

Generally, while you say you are fine when you're not, your facial expressions can display what you truly feel at the moment. Facial expressions reveal what you are trying to hide without you being aware of it. You may try to fake a smile, but you can't hide the pain in your eyes when you are hurt emotionally.

Here some examples of emotions that can be apparent in your facial expressions:

- Anger
- Surprise
- Disgust
- Hatred
- Fear
- Anxiety
- Confusion
- Excitement
- Desire
- Contempt

Disbelief and doubt can also be detected via facial expressions. A study revealed that a trustworthy person slightly raises their eyebrows along with a slight smile that conveys confidence and friendliness.

Among the various forms of body language, facial expressions are among the most universal. Expressions conveying fear, loneliness, anger, and happiness are the same.

Paul Ekman, a researcher, disclosed that we make judgments about people's intelligence based on what's shown across their faces. One study indicated that people with narrower faces and prominent noses are perceived to be intelligent. Those with cheerful expressions are bound to be more intelligent than those with angry faces.

The Eyes

Often times we've heard other people referring to our eyes as the window to the soul. Maybe it's because our lips can easily tell a lie but not our eyes. Notice that when you're guilty of something, you just can't look straight into another person's face. It's because your eyes are so sensitive that they can easily convey your inner feelings.

When you are engaged in a conversation with another individual, looking to their eyes is natural and significant to the process of communication. If you take note of the eye movement, you can see if the person you are talking to is:

- Averting their gaze
- Making direct eye contact
- Blinking their eyes

People may also have dilated pupils.

Pay Attention to the following signals:

Eye Gaze

A person who looks directly into your eyes while talking to you shows interest and is paying attention. However, prolonged eye contact can be disturbing and threatening. Breaking eye contact or trying to avert your gaze away from the person you are talking to can indicate that you are distracted or uncomfortable or it could be that you are concealing certain emotions.

Blinking

It's natural to blink your eyes once in a while but not too little or too much. People who are distressed or uncomfortable often blink their eyes but those who blink less frequently try to control their blinking to contain excitement. Poker players often use this technique so they can appear to be disinterested to their opponents.

Size of the Pupil

This can be a very subtle form of nonverbal communication. Though the level of lighting controls pupil dilation, there are times when emotion can cause a small change in the eye.

Have you ever heard the term "bedroom eyes?" People use this expression to indicate a desirous or sexually aroused look. On its lighter side, it is the kind of look that a man or women uses when they are interested in someone.

The Mouth

Another physical aspect that is significant in reading body language is the mouth. Habits like chewing on the bottom lip can show that the person is worried, insecure, fearful or anxious. Even smiles can be interpreted in many ways. A person can have a genuine smile or smile to cover up a feeling. Smiles can also be a sign of cynicism.

When you cough or yawn, your hand automatically covers up your mouth. Nonetheless, there are people who do this as an attempt to cover any facial expression showing disapproval.

When trying to assess a person's body language, pay attention to the following lip and mouth signals:

- Pursed lips
- The tightening of the lips means distrust, dislike, and disapproval
- Biting the lips indicates being stressed, worried, or anxious
- A mouth that is either turned up or down can indicate what a person is feeling at the moment. If the mouth is vaguely turned up, it is an indication of happiness. However, when the mouth is slightly turned downward, it means that a person is sad. This can also be a sign of disapproval or an outright grimace.

This is the clearest and obvious of all body signals. It is common to see someone waving, pointing or raising a hand to get someone's attention. Using hands to indicate numbers is also widely used all over the world and it is easily recognized by people in the different regions, states, or countries.

There are some cultural signs that are considered a positive sign in one region but abominable to others. An example of this is the circling of the thumb and index finger as a sign of money. It is not appropriate to use this hand signal when you are in Japan or in the Middle East countries as they consider it an abominable behavior.

Here are some common examples of hand signals and their meanings.

- The "OK" gesture is indicated by having your index finger and thumb touch each other forming a circle while the remaining fingers are extended. This means that you're okay. However, in some places in Europe, this can mean that you're nothing and the same signal is, likewise, considered vulgar in some parts of South America.
- A clenched fist can be a sign of anger or it can mean solidarity to some.
- The "V" sign that is made by lifting your index finger and middle finger and separating them to create a V-shape can either mean peace or victory in some countries. However, when the hand is facing outward, it can be offensive to Australians.

Arms and Legs

- Defensiveness can be shown by crossing the arms while crossing legs away from another person may show discomfort or dislike.

- Standing with hands on your hips is a sign of readiness and being in control though it can, likewise, be a sign off aggressiveness or being boastful.
- Clasping your hands behind your back indicates that you are bored, angry, or anxious.
- Restless tapping of fingers or fidgeting can signal that a person is frustrated, impatient or bored.
- Crossed legs mean that you are feeling closed off or in need of a little privacy.

How we sit, stand or hold our bodies can also tell a lot about us. Posture is our overall physical form and how we hold it. By merely looking at one's posture, you can determine a lot of information about how the person is feeling, their personality and characteristics - e.g., if the person is confident, shy, open or submissive.

- Sitting with the body hunched forward indicates that a person is bored and indifferent to their surroundings.
- When trying to read signals coming from an individual's posture, take note of the following:
    - When a person is sitting up straight, it means that they are a serious individual,

focused, and paying attention to what's going on around them.

- An open posture or the kind that keeps the trunk of the body open and exposed indicates openness, friendliness, and willingness. Closed posture, on the other hand, is where the trunk of the body is hidden because it is hunched forward hunching with the arms and legs crossed. This indicates unfriendliness, hostility, and anxiety.

Do you feel uncomfortable when someone comes too close to you?

There are people who don't want their personal space invaded by others. When someone comes too close for comfort, they feel uncomfortable.

Edward T. Hall, an anthropologist coined the term *proxemics,* which refers to the distance between people while in an interaction. Just when facial expressions and gestures tell much about a person, so does the physical space between two individuals.

Hall described the four levels of social distance that occur in different situations:

Intimate Distance (6-8 Inches Apart)

This distance indicates a closer relation or intimacy between two people where there is greater comfort involved. This can occur when two people are in an intimate position like hugging, kissing whispering, and touching.

Personal Distance (1.5 - 4 Feet Apart)

This indicates the level of distance between family members and close friends. The closer the distance that two individuals can interact comfortably indicates the level of intimacy in their relationship.

Social Distance (4-12 Feet Apart)

This is applicable to the distance between acquaintances. For someone you know fairly well like coworkers, you may be more comfortable interacting at a closer distance but for those you seldom see, a bigger distance can be more acceptable.

Public Distance (12-25 Feet Apart)

This range of physical distance is commonly used in public speaking. Talking to a large audience or giving a presentation at work is an example of this.

The level of distance that affects an individual's sense of comfort can vary with culture. This is the reason why we can experience culture shock from time to time when we travel abroad or even in another town far from where we live. Those living in Latin countries would find it more comfortable to get closer to one another while interacting but North Americans need more personal distance.

Chapter 5: The Language Differences in Sexes

Ever wondered if males and females have the same body language? To answer this, let's study their language cues.

Men are not as good as women in reading body language although they use different parts of their brains in doing so. According to Monica Moore from Webster University in St. Louis, men often miss a woman's first courtship signal. Usually, it takes a woman to eye-gaze three times before a man noticed her.

Moreover, women are better at reading body language because more of their brain cells are active every time they evaluate other behaviors. MRIs, likewise, revealed women have 14-16 active areas in the brain while studying other people's behavior while men only have 4-6.

When it comes to lying, men are motivated differently from women. While men lie to appear more successful, interesting, and powerful, women lie to protect others. They also lie about themselves. Men lie eight more times about themselves than women do.

Men's Body Language

If you know what you're looking for, the body language of a man is easier to read. Men have a certain way of standing, eye gazing, gesturing or shaking with their hands that will give you an idea about their real emotions and character.

Most often men think that they can fool people around them by showing them the behavior they are exhibiting. However, most of the time, they don't realize that their body language definitely exudes subtle signals for other people to see. Most of men's body language is hidden from them. So, if a person is trying to appear confident, their body language may show the opposite.

Studies on men's body language vary but have one point in common, which is the fact that body language makes up 50 - 80 of our communications. They also agree that there is body language that is common across all cultures.

Now, let's focus on the body language of men in particular. Studies show that conversation for men is largely a reflexive movement that does require much thought. However, some men have successfully learned to use body language and consciously use it to project the behaviors they want to convey to others.

Dominance

Men learn to project a dominant stance by standing with their shoulders squared off and hips facing forward with hands down at the sides. This shows that the man is extremely confident and, therefore, feels more dominant over another person. This stance can be used with intent when a man wants to exert dominance over someone.

Aggressiveness

With legs closed together and weight pushed forward, a man can have an aggressive stance. This can include shifting the dominant foot forward by about half a step. The head and chin might be slightly tilted forward or off-center.

Once the man takes this stance, it indicates that he is ready to fight - verbally or physically.

Being Defensive

When a man feels threatened, worried or fearful, he can easily move to the defensive stance. Here are a series of movements usually associated with the defensive stance:

- Feet turned outward
- Arms held close to the body
- Shoulders hunched

- Hands clasped in front
- Arms crossed over the chest or stomach

A man may resort to a defensive stance when they are feeling that they will be verbal or physical attacked by the person they are talking to.

Open Palms or Hiding the Palm

An open palm in men is a sign of openness, trust, and sincerity. It's like saying, I truly mean what I say. Having an open palm is a way of showing people that you are not holding any weapon that can harm anyone – literally or figuratively. This form of body language is often used by politicians.

Conversely, closing the hands into a fist conveys aggressiveness or being in a defensive position. If the palm of your hand is hidden like in a closed fist, you are trying to show dominance over another person or you could be defending someone.

Touching the Face

When men touch their face while talking, it is a sign of dishonesty or anxiety. Most gamblers use a poker face, but they can't help touching their faces when bluffing. Even politicians do this when being dishonest. Some job applicants touch their faces during interviews.

Fidgeting

Fidgeting is another form of body language that differs in men and women. When men fidget, it implies boredom but when women fidget while talking, it means they are anxious about something.

Handshake

A handshake is merely a form of greeting. However, there's much that can be revealed via your handshake. The strength applied during a handshake is just as important as when you offer to shake someone's hand. Many men are concerned with the strength of their grip but if you happen to grip too hard, it could mean that you are trying to impress the other party.

Dominant Handshake

A dominant man is easily detected through a handshake. When he tries to shake your hand and their palm facing downward, it indicates that the person is trying to establish dominance over the other person and is forcing them to meet their hand. The grip is firm but not tight and done with a forward lunge. Once the grip is tightened, it can be read as aggressiveness.

Submissive Handshake

If you palm is facing upward when shaking hands, it indicates submissiveness. The one offering an upturned palm may be intimated by the person they are shaking hands with or may feel inferior because the other person is an authority figure. If you don't want to feel intimidated, make sure to use a firm grip.

Two-handed Shakes

In a two-handed shake, if the hand opposite to the one being offered in a handshake comes up to grip the shaking hand, it indicates familiarity. This shows that you are very familiar with the other person and feel equally comfortable. This handshake is usually used between two individuals who are close to each other.

Eye Language

It is often said that eyes are the windows to the soul. While you are able to control the direction of your eyes, you can't control involuntary eye movement directed by your subconscious. These eye movements show what you're thinking and feeling.

Blinking

Random blinking of the eyes is normal. However, when blinking becomes rapid, it is a sign of stress. This abnormal type of blinking may indicate that a person is worried, agitated or feeling nervous. On the other hand, blinking that is slow and deliberate can be a sign of boredom or fatigue. It can be very hard to control eye movement such as blinking and is, therefore, a good indication of a person's current mood.

Focused Gaze

When naturally focusing your gaze, particularly on the lower half of the face, is an indication that you are paying attention to what is being said. On the other hand, a focused gaze with no eye movement, where the gaze is forced, is likely to indicate that someone is pretending to pay attention but is uninterested or thinking of something else.

Wider Gaze

A wider gaze that scans the whole face using natural eye movements indicates attention to the speaker. It can also mean that someone attracted to the person who is talking.

Upper Gaze

When someone focuses their gaze on the top of the head or just above the eyes of the person they are talking to, the gazer is trying to establish dominance. Woman interpret some gazes used by men as being sexist. If this happens to you, use your hands to redirect attention. However, if the man is dominant, he will continue to look over you.

Female Body Language

The body language of women does not completely vary from that of men. Nevertheless, female body language bears some remarkable contrast that makes it easily identifiable to women.

Women exhibit different courtship behavior compared to men, particularly if they're trying to entice the person they are attracted to. Here are some samples of their notable behavior:

- **Raising of Eyebrows**

    When women are trying to attract men, they unconsciously or consciously raise their eyebrows and lower their lids at the same time. This mimics their expression when they're experiencing pleasure.

- **The "Come-Hither" Look**

The come-hither look is classic. The flirtatious glance is a woman's way to express her sexual intentions in a euphemistic manner.

- **The Sideway Glance**

The sideways glance over raised shoulders features the soft curves of a woman's face. This denotes the presence of estrogen, which signifies fertility. The gesture also releases pheromones, a hormone responsible for sexual arousal. Women instinctively glance sideways when they're trying to flirt.

- **Hair Flipping**

Women naturally toss (or flip) their hair or touch their neck when flirting. This gesture reveals the armpit and releases pheromones, highlights their crowning glory, and exposes the curvature of their neck. These factors help deepen the attraction of the opposite party.

Women sometimes find it hard to show their confidence sans intimidation. They use body cues to show vulnerability (or submissiveness) and use subtle hints of assertiveness at the same time in order to convey the silent message that their femininity does not equate to meekness.

Women usually raise their eyebrows higher to show helplessness. As a natural reaction, a man's brain secretes a hormone connected with defending or protecting the female.

When women feel confident, they stand with their feet apart. At times, they toss their hair and lift their chins up with a playful smile in their lips.

Smile

Most people assume that a smile portrays happiness. Rarely does one think that it's a sign of nervousness. Women usually hide their nervousness with a smile. You will notice this when she excessively does this even at inappropriate times.

Leaning Forward

Women lean forward when they engage in an earnest conversation. They also do this when they're flirting with somebody they like. It is important for you to take note of the key cues to accurately interpret the meaning of this particular body language.

Eye Rolling

Women usually roll their eyes out of frustration or impatience although they sometimes use this as a pretend sarcasm. When a woman stays verbally quiet and reserved but rolls her eyes, it means that she's trying to stay polite but is already losing her patience.

Eye Contact

Direct eye contact is often encouraged in Western culture. It conveys positive messages such as paying attention to the conversation and a sign of attraction. People who have a steady gaze are often perceived to be trustworthy but those who have a hard time maintaining eye contact might be a disinterested or submissive (or much worse—a liar).

However, direct eye contact is not encouraged in the East Asian culture wherein the lack of direct eye contact means reverence. Japanese women avoid looking at men to show their respect and not because she's shy or doesn't have self-confidence. Again, you have to exercise proper discretion for this particular body language.

Dilated Eyes

A woman's eyes dilate when they see something they want or like. If you've asked the woman you like for a date and her eyes dilate, you have a big chance to hear a positive reply. If you present a woman with an option she likes, you will also get this reaction.

Rapid Blinking of Eyes

Aside from circumstances when a woman is obviously flirting, rapid blinking of her eyes might mean that she's uncomfortable or nervous. If you approach a woman and she's blinking rather excessively (and not even smiling), then she's anxious or scared.

Lip Gestures

Many men think that when a woman bites her lower lip, she's seducing them. Women also do this gesture when worried, anxious or stressed out. When a woman intends to seduce a man, she will bite her lip along with an intense gaze.

When a woman tightens her lips while listening to someone, she's expressing silent but strong disapproval. She's having a hard time holding her emotions and is fighting whatever negative retort she's thinking. When women do this, it means that they intensely dislike or resent another person.

Handshake

A weak handshake indicates that a woman is nervous, shy, submissive, intimidated or a combination of all of these. On the flip side, a woman with a strong handshake means that she's confident and in control.

Hands on Hips

When men see a woman putting her hands on her hips during a conversation, it means that she's getting aggressive. By putting the hands on the hips (and sometimes with feet apart to take a wider stance), a woman unconsciously tries to get bigger; thus, looking more intimidating in the process. When the hands are clenched tight, it portrays a higher degree of hostility. A woman may be extremely difficult to placate when this occurs. If this happens, it's best to do something to break the aggression.

Exposed Wrist or Open Palm

The wrist is a vulnerable part of a woman's body just like the neck. When displayed, it signals submission. Many women unconsciously show an open palm or exposed wrist whenever they're ready to obey. She is more likely to listen to your requests or bow to your authority.

Expressive Hand Gestures

A lot of women use excessive hand gestures whenever they're completely absorbed and emotionally involved in the topic of their conversation. It's important to understand that expressive hand gestures specifically those at or above the shoulders depicts lack of emotional control. If you want to be taken seriously, limit your hand gestures or maintain them below the waist.

Locked Ankles

A woman who locks her ankles while standing or sitting might feel distressed, nervous or guilty. However, this is not true at all times as the gesture might be due to the way a woman is dressed. Women who wear miniskirts tend to cross their ankles for apparent reasons. Reserved women also have a habit of locking their ankles whenever they sit.

Chapter 6: Benefits of Knowing How to Read Body Language and Facial Expressions

Experts reveal that nonverbal cues a substantial portion of our communication. These unspoken cues actually "speak" louder than spoken words. The slightest movement of our brows or our unconscious fidgeting reveals our concealed emotions. In courtroom settings, lawyers can use nonverbal hints in order to sway the opinions of jurors. For example, the attorney may glance at his watch to convey that the opposing lawyer's argument is getting tedious. These nonverbal signals work so effectively and powerfully that some judges put limits on what types of nonverbal behavior one must observe during courtroom sessions. Let's talk more about the advantages of knowing how to read nonverbal signals.

Enhance Parenting Skills

Children are more perceptive than we think. Your body language and facial expressions can be effective when communicating with your children. You might not be aware that you're sending negative messages to your kids even without speaking them out loud. Improving your nonverbal skills can effectively boost your parenting skills in the process. Below are some examples of how you can use nonverbal communication to improve your parenting skills:

- A hug can effectively reassure a crying baby or child that everything's going to be all right.
- Taking time to listen and establishing eye contact as your child tells an important story, adventure, and school experience. Avoid multitasking because your child will think that you are not interested.
- A pat on the back (or head) or high-five shows that you're proud of your child.
- A handshake given to your teenage child means that you recognize their maturity, growth, and achievement.

Give Good Impression in Job Interviews

Observing proper nonverbal communication can be as powerful as providing the right verbal answers during a job interview. On the flip side, poor nonverbal cues might hinder an interviewee's success in the interview since they tell a lot of things about you. Arriving late for your interview symbolizes that you're an irresponsible, inefficient or simply not interested in the position you're applying for. On the contrary, being ton time conveys a positive message. Another nonverbal form of communication that you need to establish in order to make a good impression is your handshake. It should be firm and strong, lasting between three to four seconds. Make eye contact with the interviewer as you shake hands with a complete grip.

Nourish Personal Relationships

As established, nonverbal cues help you communicate various emotions to the people around you, particularly to your family. This is why unspoken rules are sometimes established. You begin to understand each other in a deeper sense. For example, one sharp look from a mother signifies that something shouldn't be done. A bubbly child's silence might mean that he or she is keeping a secret or that there might be a problem.

Identify and Read Negative Nonverbal Behavior

Having the ability to identify and understand nonverbal cues in other people will help you easily recognize negative emotions and unspoken issues.

Let's face it—we cannot avoid difficult conversations with people, whether with our family, friends, a boss, a colleague or a complete stranger. It's a painful fact of life everybody has to face at some point and time. However, it doesn't mean that you have to remain ignorant of ways on how to ease these difficult situations. You can stay composed in order to resolve the issues in a level-headed manner. But complicated feelings like anger, stress, anxiety, and defensiveness will still remain and can be reflected in our body language and facial expressions. The following behaviors show that a person is either unhappy or emotionally detached:

- The body is turned away from you
- Arms folded in front of the body
- Tense facial expression
- Downcast eyes, looking away or maintaining little eye contact

Recognizing these signs can help you easily adjust your response and how to say it in a way that won't make the situation worse or help others see your perspective.

When you need to collaborate with your team, deliver a presentation to the board or teach students, you want them to be completely engaged with you. Otherwise, you're simply wasting your time. Here are some examples that identify when your audience is bored or uninterested:

- Gazing into space or at something else

- Doodling or drawing
- Fidgeting
- Looking at phones or playing with pens
- Slouching with heads tilted down
- Picking at clothes

When you notice these signals, you can immediately do something to keep your audience engaged. For instance, you can attract their attention by asking questions or inviting them to state their own opinions or ideas.

Project Yourself Positively

Positive body language and facial expressions attract people and bring out your confidence. Below are a few tips to help you:

Observe a Positive Posture

Stand or sit straight (avoiding being stiff), with your shoulders back and arms at your sides or in front of you. Do not slouch, tilt your head downwards or put your hands inside of your pockets.

Practice Your Body Language

Look in the mirror and practice your posture. Avoid being stiff while sitting or standing. Evenly distribute your weight, keeping one foot slightly in front of the other as this will help maintain your posture.

Use Open Hand Gestures

Keep your upper arms close to your body as you spread your hands apart, palms slightly facing towards your audience. This stance shows your willingness to communicate and share ideas with your audience or the people around you. However, avoid exaggerating your gestures as people might get distracted by your movements instead of what you're actually saying.

Keep Your Head Up

Keep your head upright and level. Avoid leaning far back or forward since this makes you look arrogant or aggressive.

Have a Relaxed and Open Facial Expression

People will automatically see and feel your discomfort if you look stiff or frozen. Smile the way you would do with your friends—with warmth and sincerity. Remember, people are attracted to confident, warm, and genuine individuals.

Learning how to read and interpret these subtle hints will enable you to gain an advantage. For instance, it will help you fully comprehend the message of the person you are talking to and boost our understanding of people's reactions to what we say and do. Furthermore, you can modify your body language to appear more positive, agreeable, and appealing.

Facial Profiling

Facial profiling is identifying a person's personality by analyzing their facial features. It is a form of physiognomy, the concept that one's personality can be gauged through the analysis of his or her facial features. According to accumulated research in the field of social and life sciences, personalities are affected by our genes and our face is a reflection of our DNA. There are no clear, solid pieces of evidence that directly identify physiognomy as a reliable tool but recent studies have suggested that analysis on facial appearance contains a relevant amount of truth about a person's personality and character.

Reading faces can be a vital skill particularly when you meet and communicate with a lot of people on a daily basis. You will have the ability to take care of the people closest to you, have a better understanding of your co-workers and clients, and gauge the hidden emotions of the people you come in contact with.

So, how do you read and analyze facial features to determine the personality of a certain individual? For starters, you have to consider the following elements:

- Face shape, ears, and hair
- The shape and size of the lips, mouth, and chin
- Length and shape of the nose
- Color, size, shape, and distance between the eyes and eyebrows
- The type and size of the forehead including the wrinkles and their alignment

Face Shape

Oval

People with an oval-shaped face are sweet, charming, and have a balanced personality, which is why they're often the best pacifiers or diplomats. Women with oval faces in particular, are often the best artists. These people can also be phlegmatic and inactive.

Round

This is also known as a water-shaped face since the face is normally plump. These people are known to be empathetic and caring. They also have strong sexual fantasies. If you desire a long-term relationship, people with round faces can be a great choice.

Oblong

People with an oblong-shaped face have cheekbones not wider than their jawline and forehead. They are usually practical, organized, and are workaholics. They also have a strong inclination to narcissism and problematic relationships.

Rectangle

Rectangular-faced individuals can also be domineering but not as much if compared to their square-faced peers. They're also active in the field of sports, politics, and business. They are usually ambitious and melancholic.

Square

People with a square-shaped face are highly analytical and intelligent. They have decisive, aggressive, and dominating personalities.

Diamond

This face shape is characterized by prominent cheekbones, a pointed chin, and a regular nose. They are confident, perfectionists, and determined. These qualities make them good leaders. On the other hand, they can be unpredictable and quick-tempered. They usually have problematic relationships and achieve success late in life.

Triangle

People with triangular face have a wide forehead, straight cheekbones that taper from the jawline to the forehead, and a square and/or flat chin. They are active but have low stamina. They are highly intelligent, creative and vivacious although they easily get depressed, emotional, and sensitive.

Heart or Inverted Triangle

Heart-shaped faces are characterized by large foreheads and a V-shaped jawline. These people are great in self-analysis, quick-thinking, and have a good memory. They also love independence, sincerity, and commitment. They are very ambitious by nature.

Hair

Black

People with straight black hair are usually calm, melancholic, and pessimistic. On the other hand, curly-haired ones are genial, affectionate, and positive.

Blond

This hair color reflects obedience, naiveté, and freshness. Blond-haired people are often physically weak but have an excellent memory. They can be impressionable and indifferent at the same time.

Brown

Generally, people with brown hair are quite romantic but indifferent at times. They love to travel and experience adventures. They have strong character and radical ideas. Those with dark brown, silky hair can be seductive, sensible, proud, confident, and sociable. Those with coarse brown hair are independent, resilient, hardworking, reliable, and responsible. They are exemplary in handling finances.

Red

People with dark red hair are usually temperamental, skeptical, quarrelsome, and courageous. They are often endowed with great physical prowess. Bright red-haired individuals have sensitive, intelligent, and lustrous spirits. Those with silky hair have a loving and passionate nature. If red-haired people have fair skin, they often have a high artistic sense and are highly imaginative.

Hairy People

Men who have hairy bodies can be sentimental. They are also strong and energetic, leading them to excel in sports. On the contrary, those who have no hair can be cunning, clever, and dominating. They also have high business acumen.

Eyebrows

Straight

People with straight brows are direct, technical, and realistic. They appreciate logic and need to be presented with facts and relevant data in order to be thoroughly convinced. They can also separate their emotions so that their judgment won't be clouded.

Curved

This means that a person is people-oriented. People with curved eyebrows have the ability to relate and connect to the world through their understanding of people. They are quite pragmatic and learn best through personal experiences. They hate technical details and theories but prefer the practical approach instead.

Angled

People with angled eyebrows stay calm in any given situation. They are gregarious and have great leadership qualities. They are usually mentally focused and often do the right thing.

Low

Expressive and impulsive—that's how people with low eyebrows are. They can quickly assess and process information; hence, they also have the ability to make snap decisions. They are "doers" instead of "thinkers" and want to get the job done right away. Moreover, these people tend to be optimistic at first but become antagonistic when criticized. They lack patience and are always on-the-go.

High

High eyebrows denote discerning. These people take their time to observe and sort out their ideas before actually acting on a certain situation. They need thorough information in order to deeply understand a subject, a mystery, or a puzzle. They store information with an emotional mark so that when they recall the feeling or emotion, they can automatically remember the event or information with great clarity. They find it hard to make snap decisions or assessments as they always need time to reflect on matters.

Bushy

Bushy brows denote great intellectual capacity. These people never run out of ideas as they are mentally active.

Winged

Winged brows are characterized by a thick beginning and a thinner end. These people are great planners as they always come up with huge new ideas. They are visionaries, allowing them to create new challenges. However, they can be quite weak in follow-throughs.

Pencil-Thin

People with fine-lined brows are often associated with single-mindedness. They can only focus on a certain thing at a time. They also tend to be overly sensitive or self-conscious and can be people-pleasers.

Even

This brow type has the same thickness all throughout its length. People with even brows possess mental clarity. Ideas tend to flow smoothly and consistently, making it easier for these people to grasp whole concepts. They tend to be intolerant of "slow" people or those who can't instantly get their ideas.

Managerial

Managerial brows are characterized by a thin beginning and thicker outer edges. People who possess this brow type can do great follow-through. They are well-organized and methodical, making them the right people in roles that require meticulous attention and detailed work.

Access

Characterized by hairs growing straight at the beginning of the brows, these people have a deep and strong connection between their logical mind and inner emotions. They can instantly pinpoint potential problems. Those who only have excess hair on the right brow mean that they can spot dilemmas in the field of business. If it's on the left, they can predict or anticipate probable complications within a relationship.

Tangled or Wild

Wild brows indicate unconventional thinking. These people can see and assess the various facades of a certain issue. They have the ability to play the devil's advocate and unravel hidden truths and mysteries. Their unusual way of thinking also attracts unwanted trouble or conflict.

Chameleon or Nearly Invisible

These people are known to have the ability to easily blend into any group. They are great negotiators and can be great spies since they have the talent to extract information from certain people.

Eyes

Black

Black eyes convey mystery and secrets. People with black eyes are often secretive but trustworthy. They are also practical, optimistic, passionate, and charismatic. Most of them are also natural-born leaders.

Brown

Individuals with brown eyes are energetic, creative, courageous, persistent, and productive. They don't value material gains too much. Instead, they focus their attention on nature, spirituality, and freedom.

Hazel

This color is actually a mixture of green and brown. Hazel-eyed people are brave, independent, sensible, and spontaneous. If the brownish shade is more abundant, it means that the person is approachable.

Gray

Grey-eyed people are sensitive, have great analytical prowess, and possess a great deal of inner strength. They are also versatile as they can easily switch their moods to suit the present situation.

Blue

Blue eyes are considered to be most desirable as most people associate this eye color with eternal youth. People with light blue eyes have the tendency to be competitive, skeptical, and egocentric. On the other hand, those with darker shades are often more agreeable.

Green

According to a study, green eyes are often connected to sexiness and creativity. Green-eyed people also resort to underhanded tactics.

Monolid

People with single-fold eyelids tend to be logical, rational, and stubborn. They also have the ability to manage their finances wisely.

Double-Fold Eyelids

Those with double-fold eyelids are often emotional, sentimental, impulsive, bold, and eccentric. They can be flexible and talented when it comes to acquiring financial resources. Unfortunately, they also have a weak sense of handling their finances.

Hooded Eyes

Hooded eyelids are depicted as being partially covered by skin that drops down from the brow bone, making one look sleepy. These people possess the characteristics that both monolid and double-folded eyelid people have. They have an implicit and temperate style and can be reserved. They work carefully but seem to lack in spirits so only a few of them tend to become leaders.

Other Attributes

People with large, round eyes are usually flirty and affectionate. They are intelligent, imaginative, and quite impulsive. If there's a big space between the eyes, it means that you prioritize honesty and simplicity. If their eyes are close together, they are focused but can also be restless.

Individuals with small eyes are observant, cunning, and malevolent. They are opportunity seekers and tend to take advantage even of the smallest things.

People with a closed set of eyes have the talent to quickly learn foreign languages. They also have a good memory.

Nose

Aquiline

Those with an aquiline nose have a commanding personality. They are proud and determined. However, if the nose is too narrow, the person can be rather dictatorial.

Straight

People with a straight and proportioned nose tend to be patient, kind, elegant, and persevering. They have well-balanced personalities although they can also be cold and indifferent at times. They usually have liberal ideas in areas of moral and social aspects of life.

Meanwhile, those who have a straight nose with the nose tip bent downwards are usually melancholic and lenient.

Pointing Up and Slightly Curved In

These people are often enthusiastic and skillful. They can efficiently implement their strategies despite the obstacles. They are always cheerful, stylish, and optimistic about their goals. One can't be mad at them for too long due to their nature.

Snub

People with a snub nose often display dominance and lack of elegance in many aspects of life. However, they can be eloquent speakers and have literary and poetic prowess.

Curved

A curved nose exhibits sharpness, indifference, and hostility. Partnered with thin lips and bent mouth edges, it conveys that the person is gossipy.

Cheeks

Fleshy or Meaty

People with fleshy cheeks are usually artistically inclined and have a special sensitivity.

Round and Full

Those with round cheeks are innocent and languid.

Sunken

Sunken cheeks are often associated with people who are morose, depressed, and often sick.

Extra Smooth

Those who have very smooth cheeks are usually carefree.

Furrowed

People with furrowed cheeks are simple and unsophisticated. They are also happy workers but are not workaholics.

Raised to the Eye

These people are warm, generous, compassionate and sympathetic. Their ultimate weakness is being receptive since they lack critical ability.

Lips

Thick

Thick lips are often associated with a loving character. However, if it's coupled with a split chin, it means laziness and selfishness.

Thin and Small

Those who have these types of lips are often cold, calculating, and cruel.

Pale and Tight

Accompanied by square jaws, this person is greedy, cruel, brutal, and selfish personality.

Upper Lip Partly Covers the Lower Lip

People who have this lip type are usually good-natured, loving, and favor entertainment. If the lips are thin, it signifies parsimony and selfishness.

Heart-Shaped

It conveys independence and confidence. People who have heart-shaped lips are sensual and seductive by nature.

Pronounced Lower Lip

These people can be sarcastic and highly satirical but have exemplary intelligence.

Ears

Small ears display affection, honor, and impeccable manners. If the earlobe is thick, this person is rather emotional. If the ears are too small, the person is reserved and shy. Medium ears show determination and energy.

Big ears with thick earlobes often indicate the person is materialistic and rude by nature. Distanced ears show cruelty and destructive desires.

You can determine if your ears have a normal height when they don't pass above the level of the eyebrows and are nose level. People Those with ears to past the height of the eyebrows are usually angry, vengeful, and have criminal tendencies.

People with detached earlobes are generous and free-spirited. Those with attached earlobes can be stingy and observe strict self-discipline. A large distance between the eyes and ears presents great talent and intelligence.

Forehead

A high forehead shows diligence, discipline, and success in the future. These people are scholarly.

People with a low and wide forehead are very intuitive, imaginative, and extremely talented. They love spontaneity and freedom. Their interest centers on impressions more than the knowledge gained through studies.

Meanwhile, a high and slightly wide forehead partnered with well-shaped eyebrows is the most coveted since it denotes permanent success.

A square forehead means that the person prioritizes honesty and sincerity. If it is partnered with straight eyebrows, these qualities are intensified.

A forehead lined with deep wrinkles signifies that the person indulges in deep research and contemplation. Vertical wrinkles between the eyes show that the person deeply concentrates. On the other hand, a forehead without wrinkles shows selfishness, sarcasm, and lack of empathy.

Chin

Those who have a protruding and round chin exhibit determination, prudence, wisdom, and strength. They encourage confidence through their easy and pleasant attitude.

Those who have a round dimpled chin have good business acumen.

People who have a long, square chin can be great in law enforcement and finances. However, if a person also has small tight lips, it means that they're relentless.

A bony and square chin show that they have strength of character and are slow to anger. Meanwhile, a dimply square chin shows a fiery temper and obstinate nature.

Double chin and fleshy cheeks reveal a personality that is fond of sensual pleasures and good food. These qualities are increased when a person also has large jaws.

Identifying Personality Types

Personality typing is the process of categorizing the personalities of different people according to the way they act or think. These personality types were created by Isabel Briggs Myers and Katharine Briggs in the 1960s and were based on the work of the renowned psychologist, Carl Jung. According to them, there are four key dimensions that can be utilized to classify personalities:

- Judging vs. Perceiving
- Introversion vs. Extraversion
- Sensing vs. Intuition
- Thinking vs. Feeling

Each of these four key dimensions was characterized as a *dichotomy* or a preference between two styles of being. The sum of a person's four preferred styles describes their personality type.

According to their theory, each of these dimensions were combined to generate predictable patterns in behavior and thought, so that people with the same four preferences share many attributes in how they approach their lives (e.g. common hobbies and suitable job or career).

Nothing among these personality types is considered "better" or "the best." The categorization process was mainly designed to help an individual know themselves better. It is not by any means to be taken as a tool to make someone look abnormal or dysfunctional.

Each personality type was given a letter code that stands for a preference in the manner of behaving and thinking.

Judging or Perceiving (J/P)

The dimension of Judging/Perceiving is characterized by how people deal with their lives.

Judgers prefer things to be planned and organized, considering the structure and order of the highest importance. They dislike last-minute change of plans.

Perceivers, on the other hand, value spontaneity and flexibility. They like things to be open in order to leave room for changes.

Introversion or Extraversion (I/E)

The dimension of Introversion/Extraversion depicts how an individual manages their energy.

Introverts are energized by spending time with a small group (usually family or closest friends) and feel recharged by spending time alone. They are reserved and contemplative.

Extraverts (or *extroverts*) tend to be action-oriented since they feel energized by other people or being busy. They are outspoken, expressive, and sociable.

Sensing or Intuition (S/N)

The Sensing/Intuition scale determines how a person gathers and processes information around them.

Sensors utilize their five senses and pay more attention to reality or the information they can clearly see, feel or touch, hear, smell, and taste. They are known as practical learners.

Intuitives focus more on the abstract level of thinking as they love to think about patterns, impressions, and theories. They have a creative streak and are often more apprehensive of the future than the present.

Thinking or Feeling (T/F)

The Thinking/Feeling scale focuses on how a person makes decisions based on the information accumulated by sensing or using intuition.

Thinkers place a greater emphasis on logic, facts, objective data, and sound reasoning. In short, they make decisions with their heads. They tend to be logical, consistent, and impersonal when contemplating their decisions.

Feelers prefer feelings, giving importance to their emotions so they usually decide with their hearts. Their values and principles greatly influence the decisions they make.

Each personality type is given a four-letter code which serves as an acronym for the four main dimensions of one's personality.

ISTJ (Introverted, Sensing, Thinking, Judging): The Inspector

People with ISTJ personality types love to organize and plan all the aspects of their lives particularly their family and work. They tend to be reserved, realistic, and loyal. They also place emphasis on laws and traditions, preferring to follow established rules and procedures.

Strengths

- Observant
- Realistic and Practical
- Logical
- Organized
- Detail-oriented
- Focused on the present

Weaknesses

- Subjective
- Judgmental
- Insensitive

Career Paths

Because of their nature, INTJ types tend to excel in jobs with clearly defined schedules, strong focus on tasks, and precise assignments. Popular jobs for this personality type include:

- Lawyer
- Accountant
- Detective
- Police officer
- Computer programmer
- Doctor

- Dentist
- Military leader
- Librarian

Famous People with INTJ Personalities

- Queen Elizabeth II
- Henry Ford
- US Pres. George Washington

ISTP (Introverted, Sensing, Thinking, Perceiving): The Crafter

Individuals with the ISTP personality type enjoy spending time alone whether they go on adventures, new experiences, work, or other activities. These people are passionately independent. ISTPs are also logical, rational, practical, and result-oriented. They prefer hands-on activities instead of musing on abstract ideas or concepts. They love doing new things and tend to quickly get bored with routine.

Strengths

- Practical learner
- Realistic and logical
- Easygoing and confident
- Cool-headed and composed

- A powerful focus on maintaining their objectivity
- Great in coping with crisis

Weaknesses

- Insensitive
- Dislikes commitment
- Thrill seekers and risk-takers
- Can easily get bored
- Difficult to read what they actually feel

Career Paths

Since ISTPs are introverted, they usually prefer to do jobs that don't necessarily require teamwork. They dislike structure but love freedom and autonomy. Since they're logical, they enjoy jobs that involve reasoning and practical experiences like:

- Forensics expert
- Engineer
- Software engineer
- Computer programmer
- Video game designer
- Law enforcer
- Scientist
- Pilot

- Firefighter

Famous People with ISTP Personalities

- Amelia Earhart
- US Pres. Zachary Taylor
- Clint Eastwood

ISFJ (Introverted, Sensing, Feeling, Judging): The Protector

ISFJ is one of the most common types of personality. People with ISFJ personalities are known to be warm-hearted and responsible. Since they are introverted, they can be quiet, reserved, and very observant. They are particularly in harmony with the emotions and feelings of the people around them.

Strengths

- Reliable
- Detail-oriented
- Perceptive
- Realists
- Practical

Weaknesses

- Neglects their own needs

- Often avoids confrontation
- Dislikes change (especially big ones)
- Disapproves abstract ideas and concepts

Career Paths

Since ISFJs stay in tune with the feelings of other people, they are effective in the healthcare industry or in jobs requiring attention to detail, planning, managing, and administering. They are highly organized, meticulous, independent, and reliable. Here are some of the ideal jobs for individuals with ISFJ personalities:

- Nurse
- Counselor
- Social worker
- Child care provider
- Bookkeeper
- Administrator
- Office manager
- Teacher
- Banker
- Accountant
- Paralegal

Famous People with ISFJ Personalities

- Prince Charles of Great Britain
- Louisa May Alcott
- Mother Teresa

ISFP (Introverted, Sensing, Feeling, Perceiving): The Artist

People with ISFP personalities are usually described as peace-loving, quiet, and easy-going. There are only five to ten percent of people with this type of personality.

While ISFPs can be reserved, that doesn't mean that they are cold. They're caring, peaceful, and considerate to others. Like the first three personality types, the "artists" dislike dwelling in abstract thinking and favor hands-on experiences.

Strengths

- Loyal to their beliefs, values, and principles
- Practical
- Mindful of their environment

Weaknesses

- Hates theoretical information and abstract ideas
- Intensely dislikes confrontations and arguments
- Strongly prefers to be alone

Career Paths

ISFP personalities have a strong appreciation of nature particularly animals. They go after hobbies or jobs that put them in contact with the great outdoors. Since they also love to focus on the present, they stand out in careers that exercise practicality and solve real-world problems. These jobs suit ISFPs best:

- Artist
- Designer
- Composer
- Musician
- Forest ranger
- Naturalist
- Pediatrician
- Psychologist
- Chef
- Teacher
- Veterinarian

Famous People with ISFP Personalities

- Marilyn Monroe
- David Beckham
- Auguste Rodin

INFJ (Introverted, Intuitive, Feeling, Judging): The Advocate

INFJ people are also known as the "Idealist" and are said to be one of the rarest personality types, consisting only of one to three percent of the population. They're known to be caring, gentle, and creative. Although they are often reserved, they are also highly responsive to the feelings of others. They rather enjoy thinking arcane topics and meditating about the meaning of life.

Strengths

- Idealistic
- Have strong intuition and emotional understanding
- Perceptive of the needs of other people
- Highly artistic and creative
- Future-focused
- Like abstract thinking
- Value close, deep relationships

Weaknesses

- Overly sensitive
- Stubborn
- Dislikes conflict and confrontation
- Difficult to understand at times

Career Paths

INFJs have a high artistic sense so they excel in jobs where they can express their creativity. However, their personality puts greater emphasis on deeply rooted values and convictions; thus, they can truly blossom in jobs that support these principles. They will do best in careers where they can integrate their creativity to generate significant changes in the world.

As INFJs excel in academics and their workplace, they can be perfectionists at times. They tend to be critical of themselves and strive harder in the process. Their colleagues also respect these qualities so it's only natural that they work well together. These job work best with this personality type:

- Actor
- Artist
- Writer
- Musician
- Photographer
- Counselor
- Psychologist
- Teacher
- Librarian

- Religious worker
- Entrepreneur

Famous People with INFJ Personalities

- Carl Jung
- Oprah Winfrey
- Martin Luther King, Jr.
- Taylor Swift

INFP (Introverted, Intuitive, Feeling, Perceiving): The Mediator

People with this personality type tend to be idealistic, introverted, creative, and motivated by moral values and principles. They have strong humanitarian interests and goals like making the world a better place. Moreover, they understand themselves better and know their life goals. These people search for their own purpose in life and how they can use their skills, knowledge, and talents to better serve others.

Strengths

- Devoted
- Perceptive
- Caring and have a genuine interest in others
- Puts emphasis on close relationships

- Has the ability to determine important facts and effects of a situation

Weaknesses

- Can be overly idealistic
- Difficult to understand at times
- Weak attention to details
- Has the tendency to take things personally

Career Paths

They normally do well in jobs where they can express their vision and creativity at the same time. While they can be great team players, they prefer working alone. They're passionate about defending and advocating their own set of beliefs. At the same time, they're interested in learning more about other beliefs and consider various facades of a certain issue. Below are the jobs suitable for INFPs:

- Physical Therapist
- Psychologist
- Counselor
- Social Worker
- Artist
- Writer
- Graphic Designer

- Librarian

Famous People with INFP Personalities

- William Shakespeare
- JRR Tolkien
- Audrey Hepburn

INTJ - The Architect

Also known as the "Strategist," INTJ people are highly analytical, creative, and logical. There are only one to four percent of people in the population that fall into this category.

Strengths

- Great listeners
- Love theoretical and abstract concepts
- Take criticism well
- Self-confident
- Hard-working

Weaknesses

- Perfectionist
- Tendency to be overly analytical and judgmental
- Insensitive

- Despises talk about feelings or emotions

Career Paths

INTJs are great at gathering information, analyzing it, and provide new insights. Since they value information, intelligence, and knowledge, they make exemplary scientists and mathematicians. They also excel as the following:

- Engineer
- Dentist
- Doctor
- Teacher
- Judge
- Lawyer

Famous People with INFP Personalities

- C.S. Lewis
- Hannibal
- Arnold Schwarzenegger

INTP (Introverted, Intuitive, Thinking, Perceiving): The Thinker

These people are quiet and analytical, favoring their time alone to delve deeper into abstract concepts and theories.

They never get tired of their inner world but tend to marvel in it every single time. Although they have wide social circles, they prefer to be close to a selective few. Only one to five percent of the population has this personality type.

Strengths

- Objective and logical
- Loyal and affectionate with close friends and family
- Independent
- Loves to think about abstract concepts

Weaknesses

- Insensitive
- Free-spirited
- Difficult to understand most of the times
- Easily doubts themselves

Career Paths

Since INTPs favor abstract concepts and theories, they often do well in the field of science and mathematics. Their excellent logical and reasoning skills enable them to be successful in their respective jobs.

These people give a great deal of emphasis on personal independence and autonomy. Sometimes, they clash with authority figures especially when they feel that these people suppress their ability to think and act freely. The "thinkers" shine best in these careers:

- Forensic scientist
- Geologist
- Chemist
- Physicist
- Mathematician
- Pharmacist
- Engineer
- Software developer

Famous People with INFP Personalities

- Tiger Woods
- Albert Einstein
- US Pres. Abraham Lincoln

ESTP (Extraverted, Sensing, Thinking, Perceiving): The Persuader

People who fall under this category enjoy being with their acquaintances and friends. They are conscious of details and are present-focused. When confronted with problems,

ESTPs immediately consider the facts on hand and devise a solution from them. They are also known to be "fast talkers" as they have the ability to persuade.

Strengths

- Energetic
- Has a good sense of humor
- Friendly
- Influential
- Action-oriented
- Observant
- Resourceful

Weaknesses

- Overly competitive
- Abhors monotony
- Insensitive
- Impulsive
- Insincere at times

Career Paths

ESTP are energetic individuals who dislike boredom and love being with people. Therefore, they highly favor fast-paced careers like:

- Marketer
- Sales agent
- Paramedics
- Police officer
- Entrepreneur
- Detective

Famous People with INFP Personalities

- US Pres. Donald Trump
- Thomas Edison
- Madonna

ESTJ (Extraverted, Sensing, Thinking, Judging): The Director

From the epithet, "The Director," these people like to take charge of most situations. They make sure that everything works according to the rules and regulations. They are committed to laws, traditions, and standards. They also hold strong beliefs and assume that others will do the same.

Strengths

- Realistic and practical
- Confident
- Traditional

- Have strong leadership skills
- Dependable

Weaknesses

- Inflexible and insensitive
- Bossy
- Antagonistic at times

Career Paths

ESTJs are great in supervisory roles or in careers that maintain peace and order. They strive hard to follow as well as implement the rules set by the government or society. Below are some of the most suitable careers for this personality type:

- School administrator
- Judge
- Business manager
- Accountant
- Banker
- Military
- Police officer

Famous People with INFP Personalities

- Billy Graham

- Terry Bradshaw
- Alec Baldwin

ESFP (Extraverted, Sensing, Feeling, Perceiving): The Performer

ESFPs are known to be spontaneous and outgoing. They're usually considered as class clowns and entertainers. Moreover, they're practical learners and have a great understanding of their environment.

Strengths

- Gregarious and optimistic
- Sociable
- Present-focused

Weaknesses

- Dislikes abstract thinking
- Impulsive
- Hates monotony

Career Paths

These people abhor the monotony of routine. They seek jobs that involve socializing since they feel energized being with the crowd. They find it hard to be happy in jobs that require too much structure or where you have to work alone, which is why these jobs are suitable for ESFPs:

- Actor
- Artist
- Fashion designer
- Musician
- Athletic coach
- A social worker or childcare provider
- Human resource specialist
- Counselor or psychologist

Famous People with INFP Personalities

- Pablo Picasso
- Will Smith
- Elvis Presley

ESFJ (Extraverted, Sensing, Feeling, Judging): The Caregiver

People under this category are fiercely loyal, tender-hearted, sociable, and organized. They gain energy by simply interacting with other people and they also impart their energy by encouraging others to do their best. They always think the best of others and easily give their trust.

About nine to thirteen percent of the population are considered ESFJs.

Strengths

- Gregarious
- Outgoing
- Kind and dependable
- Finds pleasure in helping others

Weaknesses

- People pleaser
- Sensitive to criticism

Career Paths

ESFJ people feel at home in the field of social and health care services or in jobs that need their support and dependability. Thus, these jobs prove to be appropriate:

- Bookkeeper
- Receptionist
- Office manager
- Childcare provider
- Nurse
- Teacher
- Social worker

- Counselor
- Physician

Famous People with INFP Personalities

- Danny Glover
- Sally Struthers

ENFP (Extraverted, Intuitive, Feeling, Perceiving): The Champion

ENFPs are described as charismatic, vivacious, and innovative. There are about five to seven percent of people that fall into this category. Furthermore, these people dislike routines and tend to focus on the future.

Strengths

- Strong communication skills
- Empathetic
- Strong interpersonal skills
- Open and fun to be with

Weaknesses

- People pleaser
- Dramatic
- Tend to overthink
- Find it hard to follow rules

- Easily stressed out

Career Paths

As mentioned, ENFPs bear a great deal of charisma and interpersonal skills. These jobs come highly recommended for this type:

- Psychologist
- Journalist
- TV Anchor/Reporter
- Politician
- Counselor

Famous People with INFP Personalities

- Dr. Seuss
- Bob Dylan
- Joseph Campbell

ENFJ (Extraverted, Intuitive, Feeling, Judging): The Giver

Strengths

- Empathetic
- Friendly and encouraging
- Organized

Weaknesses

- Overly sensitive
- Indecisive
- Approval-seeking

Career Paths

The ENFJs' strong organizational and interpersonal skills make them befitting in the following careers:

- Counselor
- Teacher
- Human resources manager
- Manager

Famous People with INFP Personalities

- Abraham Maslow
- US President Barack Obama

ENTP (Extraverted, Intuitive, Thinking, Perceiving): The Debater

ENTPs are also known as "the innovator" or "the visionary." They are expressive and clever, never running out of ideas and theories.

Strengths

- Great debaters and conversationalists
- Highly value knowledge

Weaknesses

- Unfocused
- Strongly dislike being controlled
- Argumentative
- Insensitive

Career Paths

These people are nonconformists and do their best in jobs filled with excitement and creativity. Hence, the following jobs suit them best:

- Lawyer
- Inventor or scientist
- Journalist
- Engineer

Famous People with INFP Personalities

- Walt Disney
- Alexander the Great

ENTJ (Extraverted, Intuitive, Thinking, Judging): The Commander

This personality type is quite rare, consisting merely two percent of the entire population. These people have strong verbal and decision-making skills. They also tend to focus on the future instead of the here-and-now.

Strengths

- Great in planning and organizing
- Strong leadership skills
- Assertive
- Confident

Weaknesses

- Impatient and stubborn
- Aggressive
- Intolerant

Career Paths

ENTJs strive in a work environment that requires lots of structure and lets them interact with various people. They excel in jobs where they can exercise their leadership and planning skills like:

- Entrepreneur

- Company CEO
- University professor
- Lawyer
- Business analyst

Famous People with INFP Personalities

- Bill Gates
- UK Prime Minister Margaret Thatcher
- Al Gore

Chapter 7: Learning, Recognizing, and Reading Hidden Body Messages

Body language accounts for up to more than half of how we communicate, but reading and analyzing nonverbal cues are not just about broad strokes. A certain gesture can have a number of different meanings depending on the context. Now, let's take a look at some situations where understanding these nonverbal cues or what we call body language is significant:

- Going out on a Date
- Detecting Lies
- Going on an Interview

When you are able to interpret body language accurately, you can read beyond what the other person is willing to tell you or when their words do not convey what the person honestly feels.

We lie a lot with our words. Most of the time we tell lies to save ourselves from embarrassment or penalties. Once we start telling a lie, it may lead to more lies. The lies we tell may not be big, but considered white lies, yet, we're still lying, and we willingly partake in deception from time to time to avoid conflict. However, can possibility get out of trouble with words, but our bodies are TERRIBLE LIARS! This is where reading and analyzing body language can be extremely useful when communicating with others.

When reading body language, it is your primary duty to determine whether the individual is comfortable or not in their present situation. There are many ways to determine a person's comfort level, and here are some of them:

Positive Body Language

- Relaxed and with uncrossed limbs
- Leaning closer to you
- Long periods of eye contact
- A genuine smile

Negative Body Language

- Moving or leaning away from you
- Crossed arms and legs
- Looking away
- Feet pointed towards the exit
- Rubbing or scratching the nose, rubbing the eyes or the back of the neck.

A single act can mean a thousand other things. For instance, crossed arms indicates a negative body language.

It can, likewise, tell you that the person is feeling physically cold, frustrated, or closed off. Nonetheless, it can also mean that the person may have eaten too much, and something is happening in the digestive system. It is, therefore, necessary to pay attention to multiple behavioral cues than just concentrate on a single cue as it is often misleading.

While it helps to determine a person's comfort level to accurately read their behavior, you need to look deeper. Meaning, you also have to pay attention to other cues as well as their context. As we take a look into some specific situations, we'll see how these cues will work together to help divulge the underlying truth in any given situation.

Knowing When Someone is Lying

One of the biggest benefits you can get from being able to read body language is being able to judge accurately when someone is lying. Our intuition is not 100% accurate, but with little practice, you will become more aware when someone is trying to feed you a load of crap. It's also very important that you determine what kind of lies they're telling you.

We will discuss lies that make people uncomfortable to tell the truth. With this skill, you can easily detect white lies, lies of omission, or exaggerated stories. This type of deception is very difficult to spot and so you always need to remember that regardless of what type of lies, you will never know for certain. Nonetheless, you can spot common cues that will let you know when to suspect that person is lying.

The author of the *Liespotting* conducted a study on the different ways people lie in order to determine a pattern in our body language. She was able to define through the study that liars often display much of the behavior you would find in a person who feels uncomfortable, although there are a few more additional traits.

It is said that a *Duchenne smile* or a smile that is genuine is almost impossible to fake, which is why most people end up having awkward smiles in most photos. When you think you're you have a great smile, others may think you're faking it.

A smile is seen fake if it doesn't reach your eyes. When your smile is genuine, the areas around your eyes will wrinkle because your smile automatically pushes up your cheeks and crinkles the skin near your eyes, making it hard to fake.

A real smile comes from within and shows in your eyes, which is impossible to do when you are feeling uncomfortable. It is why a non-genuine smile is a helpful way to indicate a lie.

It's a common knowledge that guilt can be seen in someone's eyes when they're lying. To overcompensate this, great liars tried their best to stay calm and offer steady eye contact. This didn't work because the liars tried not to fidget, and they stiffened their bodies.

Generally, people can't keep eye contact for long periods of time. When eye contact becomes uncomfortable, people will rub their eyes or neck and tend to look away. So, instead of exhibiting body language that implies comfort, liars would opt to do very little, which is an indicator in itself. To spot a liar, look for unusually long eye contact and tense shoulders.

Aside from all these nonverbal cues, you also need to pay attention to the context or the setting that forms the event in order to gain a full understanding of the whole situation. Liars will often offer more details than necessary, suggest punishment, and prefer to answer your question with a question, which can give them time to fabricate an answer that will hide the truth. Such behavior, when paired with the standard negative body language and cues that liars normally exhibit, will give you the right blend of behavior that should not be trusted. Separately, they won't mean much but together, they can only mean one thing - DISHONESTY.

It is important, however, to remember that there are people who are just awkward and could display such behavior. You must take into consideration the normal behavior of a person. Watch out for their eye movements and mannerisms when you know they are telling the truth and compare it to their usual responses whenever they are lying.

If you observed a lot of inconsistencies, you will know how an individual acts when they are thinking of what to say rather than recalling information. Again, this is not enough, along with anything previously mentioned to detect lies. You, therefore, have to look for multiple cues to know the difference between fact and fiction.

Reading People on a Date

Body language can be an incredible tool when you're out on your first date with someone. If you neglect to pay attention to verbal cues your date is exhibiting, you can possibly do something that will make them uncomfortable. While you may not want to go out on a date hiding the real you, starting with your best foot forward is the best way to begin any relationship in case you find out later that you are a decent match.

This requires paying close attention to your date's behavior, which is not easy when you are trying to impress your date with your charm. Nonetheless, with more practice, you'll get the hang of watching out for the right signals.

Remember that you are not looking for anything too complicated on your first date but just basic indications of comfort and discomfort. Simply put, pay attention to how your date is guarding their body. In the beginning, most people will feel fairly guarded. They will cross their arms with palms facing them and keep a reasonable amount of distance. This is quite common especially on the first date but if you like your date, your goal is to alter that body language into something more open and welcoming to ease the situation and make you both comfortable.

In some extent, we tend to mimic the behavior of others. If you feel comfortable, it will help your date change his or her behavior to match yours. This means, you should simply avoid crossing your arms and try offering a genuine smile when appropriate and feasible. Avoid distancing yourself from your date or even showing your palms to imply that you are comfortable, which will help your date be more comfortable as well.

Also, remember not to lose your patience when you detect some negative cues as levels of comfort frequently fluctuates on dates, which is usually nerve-wracking for most people. As most piano instructors will tell you on your recital, if you happen to play the wrong note, just keep going and don't worry about making mistakes. Look out for positive signs to see how your date reacts to you and focus on providing positive body language. If you continue to see negative cues, move on to another topic.

Sometimes, both of you aren't going to click and your date may exhibit many negative cues. If this happens, apply the same piano recital principle, which is to move on and don't get hung up on a problem.

Communicating Effectively in an Interview

Interviews are like first dates. You are trying to convince a person you've met for the first time to like you. However, unlike dating, an interviewer is on a different level. This alone is enough to create an environment of discomfort that can force you to display negative cues, which are not helpful. When interviewing for a job, you should avoid using body language that makes you seem closed off.

Creating a good first impression is vital in hiring decisions. So, smile pleasantly, provide a firm handshake, and properly greet the interviewer. This positive body language will set the stage for a comfortable interview that will follow. You are not aware of the expectations the interviewer will bring to the table, so it's a good idea to avoid any negative behavior by demonstrating your pleasant and charismatic personality.

Nonetheless, offering all those positive cues is easier said than done when you are feeling uncomfortable in the first place. The best thing to do is prepare before the interview. Usually, lack of preparation is the reason why people do poorly in interviews.

As preparation, research the company. An interviewer expects you to have prior knowledge of the company you want to join. Anticipate some questions that are often included in a job interview like:

- Why should they choose you over the other candidates?
- How can you help the company?
- What salary are your salary requirements?

Walking into the room with confidence is vital in creating a good first impression. Remember that you need to stand out from the crowd. When you are well-prepared to face your interview, this breeds confidence and your body automatically exhibits positive body language when you're feeling good about yourself.

While natural comfort is what you actually need, there are some tricks that can help you out when you need it. As an American cultural standard, eye contact is more important in a job interview than in most other situation. If you have trouble staring into someone's eyes, your next best option is to look at their mouth.

Like when you're on a date, leaning forward is a positive cue you can provide to your interviewer. It makes you appear a good listener even when you have to talk most of the time. When asking some questions or when your interviewer is saying something, eye contact is vital. This conveys that you are in the listening mode. Occasionally placing your hand over your mouth indicates that you aren't going to talk and are not paying attention.

The interviewer is used to small signs of nervousness and they can understand when you have it. So, when you're a bit tense on your interview, there's no need to worry about it. That is usually expected. In fact, too much comfort might convey overconfidence and not taking the interview seriously. In the end, your fate lies in the decision made by another person and there's only so much that you can do to impress the person.

They may not like the way you dress or prefer to hire someone else but with the help of your skill in reading and manipulating body language, you can at least try to tip the scale in your favor.

Reading Power Cues

Eye Contact is usually the primary way to communicate dominance. People establish dominance by taking the liberty to stare and scrutinize others while making direct eye contact. A dominant person is usually the last to break eye contact.

So, if you intend to assert your power, remember that constant eye contact can also be intimidating.

Assess Facial Expressions

A dominant person or a person in power refrains from smiling to relay seriousness. They would prefer to purge their lips instead or frown.

Evaluate Gesture and Stance

Pointing a finger at someone and using large gestures are examples of exhibiting dominance. When a person uses a taller and wider stance while being relaxed, it shows dominance.

Dominant individuals also have firm handshakes and usually place a hand on top with the palm facing downwards. The grip of this person is firm and sustained to demonstrate power and control.

Managing Personal Space

People in power or high status basically enable more physical space between themselves and people below their rank or status. This is to show dominance and mastery in every situation. Simply put, an expansive pose is a sign of power and achievement.

Power is likewise displayed in a standing position against those sitting down. Standing is seen to emit power than the sitting pose.

A straight back while keeping shoulders back instead of leaning forward further displays confidence. In contrast, slouching and slumping shows a lack of confidence.

A person of dominance also leads from the front and chooses to walk ahead of anyone especially in a group. They like to be in front and go through the door first.

The Way of Touching

Those who assert their status are likely to have more options when it comes to touching because they feel more confident of their position and authority. Generally, in a situation where two individuals have unequal status, the one occupying the higher status is likely to touch with greater frequency than the one with lower status.

Chapter 8: Knowledge and Techniques Required to Understand and Interpret Body Language

Because the majority of our communication is made through body language, it is, therefore, crucial to pay attention to it—especially when at work. This is where your emotional intelligence comes in.

How Body Language is Connected to Emotional Quotient (EQ)

Emotional Quotient is the sum of the following:

- Self-awareness
- Self-management
- Social awareness
- Relationship management

All of these elements are significant to body language.

Self-Awareness

Be mindful of your voice or tone, as well as your posture, so that you deliver the message in a way appropriate to the situation.

Social Awareness

Understanding other person's body language is, likewise, vital to how you would act in a certain situation.

Self-Management

As the situation changes, you must pay attention to the mitigating changes in your body language.

Relationship Management

This is about changing your body language and adjusting your message to suit every situation.

However, none of these is useful unless we understand the meaning behind the body language. Here is some of the common body language often used in the workplace:

Confident

- Face is relaxed
- Solid eye contact
- Firm handshake
- Walking with purpose
- Hand movements are wide and open
- Arms open

Nervous or Uncertain

- Face tight and tensed
- Avoid holding eye contact
- Movements of the hands are jerky
- Arms are folded across chest
- Walking is not stable or tentative
- Handshake is weak

Defensive

- No eye contact, eyes are downcast
- Hand gestures are closer to the body
- Arms crossed or folded over chest
- Facial expression is neutral
- The body is turned away from you

Bored and Inattentive

- Head is down
- Glazed eyes
- Slumped when sitting in a chair
- No eye contact; Eyes are somewhere else
- Hands are fidgeting
- Thinking (Prior to responding)

Thinking (Prior to Responding)

- Head tilted on an angle while eyes looking at a distance
- Hand on the cheek
- Fingers are either resting on the chin
- Broken eye contact. Eyes return only when something is asked

Harvard psychologist, Amy Cuddy, researched the impact of body language on an individual's confidence, influence, and success. Her findings dwell on the potent effects of positive body language.

Studies show that people with positive body language are more competent, persuasive, likable, and possess a higher level of emotional intelligence.

Let's find out how positive body language works.

It Changes Behavior and Attitude

Cuddy suggests that adjusting your body language to make it more positive has a powerful impact on your hormones, which improves your attitude.

It Increases Testosterone

When thinking of testosterone, you are probably thinking more of those manly hormones commonly used in competitive sports. However, testosterone is more than sports. In fact, it covers much more. Testosterone works to improve anyone's confidence—in both men and women, which causes other people to see you as someone who is positive and trustworthy. Research also proves that positive body language increases your testosterone levels by 20%.

It Decreases Cortisol

Another stress hormone that impedes performance and creates negative effects on your health over time is cortisol. By decreasing levels of cortisol, it minimizes stress and enables you to have a clear mind particularly when facing challenging and difficult situations. Studies, likewise, prove that positive body language decreases cortisol levels by at least 25%.

It Creates a Powerful Combination

While increased testosterone and decreased cortisol can do wonders on their own, when combined, it results in a powerful combination that is often found in people who are in a position of power. This combination creates confidence and clarity of the mind that is a significant requirement for dealing with pressure brought on by tight deadlines, making tough decisions, and massive workloads.

People who have high testosterone levels and are low in cortisol are known to survive under pressure. You can develop positive body language even when you don't have these natural gifts.

It Makes you More Likeable

Body language is a big factor in how you are perceived by others and is more important than your voice, tone, or the message you're trying to impart. Using positive language, therefore, can influence people to like and trust you more.

Ways to Gauge EQ Through Body Language

Now that you are aware of how EQ is strongly linked to body language, you can see how EQ development is essential to acquire a set of positive body language that can help you achieve a better, happier, and successful life in the future.

Our body contains thoughts as well as emotions and conveys messages that other people pick up to use and make judgments on us. Becoming aware of those messages that our body is sending is crucial to our success in all areas of life. By being aware of what our body does, we can manipulate the messages that it is sending so that they will cause the impact we intend.

Here are ways emotional intelligence is conveyed in body language:

Handshakes

Handshakes are basically important as they leave indelible impressions of us to others. A handshake that is weak leaves an impression of a lack of confidence and interest. Conversely, bone-crushing handshakes send red flags of an aggressive individual with the tendency to be dominant. When doing a handshake, meet the other person's eyes when possible as this can leave a lasting impression. People with high EQ know the right amount of pressure to use appropriately in every situation.

Giving Appropriate Space

The amount of appropriate space where one can be comfortable varies in every culture. If you stand too close to a person you just met, it can be uncomfortable for them and emits a signal of aggressiveness and dominance while standing too far from the person is a sign that you are uncomfortable with the person or you lack the confidence you need.

Facing Others Squarely

When you aren't squaring your body when conversing or turning away from the person you are speaking to indicates that you are either uninterested or uncomfortable. This can be a sign of disrespect or being impolite.

Positive body language involves parallel shoulder and foot placement mirroring that of the other person. People who have high EQ levels usually lean towards the person they are talking to. This means that they are giving them their complete and undivided attention.

What Posture Suggests

Standing straight or sitting up while speaking is a power position. They are an indication of confidence and self-respect as well as showing interest in what the other person is saying. Simply put, they value the conversation.

On the other hand, slouching indicates the opposite such as the lack of serious intent on whatever the other person is saying. It also suggests that you don't care how the other person views you; it can be a sign of a lack of self-esteem.

Shutting Out Distractions

We have experienced at one time or another a person who is checking their watch or mobile phone while engaging in a conversation. This makes us want to end the discussion. It is apparent that the other person is not interested in whatever it is that you're saying and has a more interesting thing to do than listen to you. People with high EQ are constantly on guard against this kind of behavior and the message it implies. To avoid this, fight the habit to look at your watch or device when you are talking to someone.

Appropriate Eye Contact

Failing to have eye contact can arouse suspicion that you are hiding something. Looking down when someone is telling you something can be regarded as a lack of confidence or interest. However, intense, sustained eye contact implies aggressiveness or wanting to dominate although there are cultural variations. Those with great EQ levels, however, tend to maintain eye contact for a few seconds to convey respect for the other person and keep the conversation focused. It is vital to glance to the side instead of the floor to avoid being perceived as uninterested.

Unconscious Microexpressions

A smile to start up a conversation can warm the heart but when it's unnatural, it may cause suspicion as well as question the sincerity of the person.

A pleasant neutral expression is much better than forcing a smile you don't feel. Scowling or having a serious expression can convey hostility causing others to get defensive and uncomfortable.

Having the right body language is just as important as using words with the appropriate tone of voice when speaking to others. Just like any other habit, it comes down to practicing until it becomes natural as you acquire the skill.

Chapter 9: Reading and Understanding Different Cues

Reading nonverbal behavior is a complex task since it involves people and every individual is unique and presents themselves differently. The task of reading body language can be challenging because you are trying to interpret the signs sent by people. One can't read and understand what's behind a certain action without taking into account the whole picture.

In interpreting other people's body language, you have to take into account the following:

- Personality
- Social factors
- Verbal behavior
- Setting

While the information presented isn't always complete and in some other circumstances not available, reading body language can be useful. Because people are complex, it shouldn't come as a surprise that the way they convey themselves through their bodies.

The Mouth

Another physical aspect that is significant in reading body language is the mouth. Habits like chewing on the bottom lip can show that the person is worried, insecure, fearful or anxious. Even smiles can be interpreted in many ways. It can be a genuine smile, or an attempt to cover up the person's real feeling. It can also be a sign of cynicism.

Once you feel that you are about to cough or yawn, your hand automatically covers your mouth. Nonetheless, there are people who do this as an attempt to cover any facial expressions showing disapproval.

When trying to assess a person's body language, pay attention to the following lip and mouth signals:

Pursed Lips

- The tightening of the lips is evident of distrust, dislike, and disapproval.
- Biting the lips indicates being stressed, worried, or anxious
- The mouth that is either turned up or down can be a sullen indication of what the person is feeling at the moment. If the mouth is vaguely turned up, it is an indication of happiness. However, when the

mouth is slightly turn downward, it means that the person might be sad. It can also be a sign of disapproval or an outright grimace.

Gestures

This is the clearest and obvious of all body signals. It is common to see someone waving, pointing or raising a hand to get someone's attention. Using hands to indicate numbers is also widely used all over the world and it is easily recognized by people in the different regions, states, or countries.

There are some cultural signs that are considered a positive sign in one region but abominable to others. An example of this is the circling of the thumb and index finger as a sign of money. It is not appropriate to use this hand signal when you are in Japan or in the Middle East countries as they consider it an abominable behavior.

When it comes to reading body language accurately, you need to consider individual differences. There's no one-size-fits-all policy. Hence, if you are interested in studying an individual, you need to take some time to do it. What holds true for one person may not necessarily hold true to another.

For instance, it is a common for liars to avoid eye contact because of guilt. This may be true to some but there are people who manage to master this skill to get away with telling lies.

Body language varies according to culture.

- In the Finnish culture, making eye contact symbolizes that a person is easy to approach. In contrast, Japanese culture this is an expression of anger.

- Westerners easily lean forward and square their faces and bodies towards you when they are comfortable.

- Autistic people also have their own unique body language. When listening, they avoid eye contact and play with their hands.

While body language differs from culture to culture, there are certain nonverbal expressions that are universal and common to all cultures like smiling to signify friendliness and a lowered posture to indicate submission.

Understanding body language differs according to nonverbal communication channels. The nonverbal channel refers to the means by which a cue or message is relayed without the use of words. Significant nonverbal channels include those of kinesics (eye contact, body language, and facial expressions), haptic (touch), and proxemics (personal space). In simple words, it's the medium that determines the message.

As a general rule, people can easily read facial expressions, and then body language, before personal space and touch. Even within the same channel, there are variations. To illustrate, not all facial expressions are easy to read and understand. People are generally better at reading pleasant facial expressions than unpleasant ones. There is a study that stated individuals are better in accurately reading contentment, happiness, and excitement compared to disgust, fear, and sadness.

In interpreting verbal and nonverbal cues, you want to read a person beyond what you can see. Logic alone won't tell you the whole story of what is behind a person's facade. You must learn to surrender to other vital forms of information so you can learn to read and understand the important non-verbal intuitive cues that people emit unconsciously. To do this, you need to rid yourself of any preconceptions and emotional baggage such as resentments, prejudice, or clashes of ego that hinders you from seeing someone clearly.

While reading other people—your partner or anyone with accuracy, keep away from biases. Regardless of how brilliant the intellect is, you have to let go of limiting ideas. People trained to read others are trained to read what is unseen or invisible so they can utilize their super senses. Most of the time, this requires surrendering pure logic in favor of receiving non-linear forms of alternative inputs.

Here are useful body language techniques in reading cues.

In this technique, try hard not to read body language cues and try not to be intense or analytical. Instead, stay relaxed and fluid. Be comfortable, simply sit back and observe.

Focus on the Person's Appearance

- Take note of the style and color of the clothes they're wearing
- Do they dress for success?
- Do they dress for comfort?
- Do they dress for seduction?
- Are they wearing anything to indicate spiritual values like a cross pendant?

Notice the Posture

When trying to analyze posture, take note of the following:

- Do they hold their head high? (confidence)
- Do they walk with indecisive steps? (low self-esteem)
- Do they swagger when they walk (arrogance)

Analyze Body Expressions and Facial Expressions

Isn't it interesting how two people can converse without actually speaking? Body language has played an important role especially in the world of dating. The laws of attraction revolve around body language. A man and a woman can express their attraction to the opposite sex through physical action or gestures and facial expressions.

Emotional Cues

Noticing the signals that other people are sending and accurately understanding them is a very useful skill one needs to learn. With a little sensitivity, attentiveness, and practice you can develop this habit and it can become second nature to you.

Crying

Crying is the same across all cultures. It is a sign of sadness or grief. At times, crying can also be a sign of joy and happiness. Crying is sometimes associated with laughter. So when evaluating crying, you need to look for other signals to determine its appropriate context.

While emotions can be manipulated in general, so is crying to gain sympathy or as a tool for deception. We call this "crocodile tears"—a colloquial term that draws on the myth that crocodiles do cry when catching prey.

Anger or Threat

When you see a person with eyebrows drawn in a V-shape accompanied with wide eyes and a down-turned mouth, expect that person to be angry.

Other signs common in an angry individual are arms tightly crossed and the person being closed off.

Anxiety

A person suffering from anxiety can be detected by fidgeting hands that they can't seem to control or keep in place. This person also unconsciously taps their feet to cope up with the feeling of restlessness.

Embarrassment

When a person is embarrassed, they tend to avert their eyes, and turn their head away with a controlled or a tense smile.

If a person is timid and shy, they may focus their attention on the floor. People who are upset also behave this way when trying to hide an emotion. When they are thinking or experiencing unpleasant emotions, they tend to stare at the ground.

Proud or Boastful

People display pride by smiling a little with the head tilted backward, and hands on their hips.

Attraction Cues

When a group of people were asked about the best tip on flirting, their answer was reading body language. So now, let's focus on the common attraction cues usually evident in women.

A woman that draws attention to her lips is indeed sending a strong sensual signal. This can be her subtle way of telling the guy how he strongly attracts her. Other cues may involve wetting her lips, eating something slowly or putting on lipstick. Through this body language, she is saying that she wants to have some fun with you.

Another indication that a woman is sexually interested in you is when she is playing with her glass using her fingers. Usually, this occurs in bars or night clubs. It is not just a habit but a form of teasing or tempting the man.

When a woman swings her legs while sitting cross-legged, it indicates that she is in a sexual mood.

However, there is unconscious body language and women may not be aware they are sending a sexual cue. This occurs a woman claspes her hands and places them over her stomach. It is a way of telling others that she is fertile and ready to conceive.

When women are showing you positive signs of sexual attraction, she can, likewise, send out cues to show disinterest in an individual. When women talk to you with arms crossed, this means she is not interested in you or in having a conversation with you. They are crossing their arms over their chest because they feel threatened, which means she has a preconceived idea of distrust towards you.

If women are sending sexual cues, what about guys? Are they sending the same cues?

The answer is YES! Men, like women, know how to use different body language and the most common one is inserting a thumb in their pants pocket or placing their hands over the crotch of their pants. Unconsciously, men are showing off their crotch area to attract potential sexual mates.

Another indicator of attraction is the seating position. You may not be aware of it, however, in a large group of people, we can identify who we are attracted to if our bodies are facing the person. Even when someone else engages us in a conversation, we simply turn our heads in response but retain our body position.

On the negative side, if the man chooses to play with his watch while talking with a woman, it indicates that he is forming a barrier with his arms. It could be that he finds it uncomfortable to have the woman around or he could also be nervous engaging with her. So for women, I suggest that you try to be a bit more friendly and lively when you find your date acting this way.

There are countless body languages used for flirting and both men and women are using them in their everyday life. Learning how body language can help you find a romantic partner proves to be useful most of the time.

Relational Cues

Body language can say much about what's happening in a relationship. Whether one partner is feeling distant, having second thoughts about something, or will is excited to go home to be with you.

The clues are actually written all over your partner's body language. All you need to do is to be aware of your partner's actions and be sensitive to what you have learned about nonverbal cues. Now, there's more to what you have learned in previous chapters.

Walking

When walking with your partner, you walk side by side at the same pace and if the intimacy is quite strong, it's most likely that you hold hands while walking. In psychology, when two individuals have rapport, their movements are in sync. One can, therefore, be a mirror of the other.

So when couples are walking and one is walking ahead of the other or lagging behind, it's a warning sign that they lack rapport. The one who is walking ahead means he or she wants to lead or get away from the partner or relationship while the one lagging behind is either scared of the relationship or feel intimidated by the partner. If one partner crosses the street without any verbal or nonverbal signs, it can indicate something negative.

Sitting

When sitting, intimate couples sit next to each other and not across from one another. Note that couples with positive body language make an effort to connect all the time regardless of what they are doing or where they are. Couples with good body language will face each other, have eye contact, hold hands, kiss or hug each other when not engaging in a conversation. When there are distractions, their attention is diverted but they reengage after a while. Even when eating, couples tend to eat in proportion to each other.

Negative signs are when there isn't a connection between couples. They busy themselves by reading the menu, looking out of the window, watching passersby, and using their mobile phones. Their bodies are usually angled away from each other and there is minimal body contact. One can be eating a lot while the other one is barely touching their meal. The one who barely touches the plate probably thinking of other things.

Making Love

When couples are deeply connected with each other, it can be deeper than just the physical level. There is always that strong mental connection that occurs especially when making love. Eye contact is vital—both partners should freely look into each other's eyes during lovemaking. Clasping of the hands, eye contact, touching skin to skin and kissing helps form a much deeper connection.

Conversely, negative signs in lovemaking are reflected in the closed eye as well as stiffness in the neck and shoulders. These are signs of ongoing anxiety or coldness in emotion. Sometimes, it can be a sign of guilt.

One must be aware of the nonverbal communication you receive from your partner rather than the verbal communication. According to Albert Mehrabian, a psychologist, it's not what you say that matters but how you say it.

Chapter 10: Understanding Non-Verbal Cues for Success in Career and Business

Are you aware that you have this inherent ability to see what goes on in the minds of other people? Reading other people's thoughts is not actually a magic trick but can be accomplished by deeply observing their microexpressions.

Microexpressions to be Aware of When Negotiating

Microexpressions are displays of emotions that are evidently seen through facial expressions. They occur and last for less than a second before the brain has the chance to alter the displayed emotion. Therefore, the displayed emotion is a genuine reaction to the stimulus that caused the display of emotion.

There are microexpressions that are common to everyone regardless of location. That means the reaction to a certain stimulus would be the same wherever you are or whatever culture you belong to.

Anger

It is natural for people to get upset. When a person loses control, it can turn into anger. So when in a negotiation, be mindful of the other person's temperament. Once he loses his coolness, that's the time when he becomes irritable and irrational. Manipulation can be easy at this time. So if you know how to take this to your advantage, then this can be a real opportunity for you to win the negotiation.

Fear

Fear is a sort of defense mechanism as we tend to protect ourselves although fear can be debilitating. When in a negotiation, it will be to your advantage if you can detect this sense of fear in your negotiating opponent. To use this to your advantage, you have to know what makes him fearful.

The following are apparent in a person feeling a genuine fear:

- Raised eyebrows
- Parted lips with bottom lips protruding downward

Between fear and anger, there are two major differences. The eyebrows are raised when the person is experiencing fear and lowered when angry with flaring of nostrils like an angry bull.

Disgust

When the other negotiator says "yes" to the offer but you notice that his upper lip is lifted with nose turned up in a wrinkle, then he just displayed the microexpression of disgust. You must take note of the difference between his words and his actions as his statement of agreement is not as firm as his body language indicates.

Surprise

A surprise expression can either be good or bad. A surprised expression is manifested by wide eyes, raised eyebrows, and a mouth that's partly open. Note that these are common in fear and surprise expressions.

It is important to notice if the expression of surprise is due to happy or sad expectations. If someone is extremely happy about a negotiation that you offered, scale back on your emotions. Your goal is to win the negotiation so you may have to make adjustments.

When in a negotiation, observe if the surprise act stemmed from either happy or sad expectations. When your offer proves to be too advantageous than what was expected, consider a reduction.

Contempt

This gesture is often conveyed by a sneer, e.g., with one corner of the mouth turned upward. Note that this may lead to disgust and then anger. In a negotiation, this microexpression may suggest one thing, "I am not enjoying this" or "this is insulting!"

Sadness

Dropping eyelids with lips turned down and a change in voice tone and pitch indicate sadness in the person. It could be that the person realizes that you have the upper hand and left little room to negotiate. If this is the case, you should avoid turning sadness into anger, which may eventually lead to a negative response.

Happiness

This is evident in a person's smile, wide-eyes, raised cheeks, and manifested gaiety.

When perceiving happiness, take note what caused it but don't let your guard down. If it's real, everything will be smooth, but it could also be an attempt to lull you into a false sense of security. Good negotiators are looking for an advantage in every negotiation and this microexpression can be the advantage you need.

When in negotiations, reading people's body language can give you insights and, therefore, be very useful. If you are able to read the thoughts and interpret your opponent's gestures, it will give you an additional advantage on the deal. Once you're able to read and analyze body language with a high degree of accuracy, you will be on your way to achieving what you have come for.

Have you ever experienced any situation when you were able to tell what someone is going to say even before words were said? How were you able to do this? You may not be aware of it, but this is actually the because your mind is mentally synchronized with another person's mind. The same thing works when someone else tells you that they have a strong feeling that you are going to say something they see in their mind. It is because your aura allows someone to hear your unspoken thoughts or see hidden chambers of your mind?

Reading Body Language to Win Negotiations

When you are negotiating, are you aware that you can negotiate better by reading the body language of the other person? The secret to reading the body language better is to know what signals to look for and how to interpret and use these signals to your advantage.

Before negotiations, take time to learn the skill of reading cues unconsciously relayed by the other party. The benefit of accurate reading and assessment of these cues can result in you winning the deal you are after.

When you are sitting at the negotiating table, allow the other negotiator to see your facade. Having the skill to read body language, likewise, provides you with the knowledge of manipulating your own body language to your advantage. When the other negotiator reads your body language the way you want them to see, they will think they have the advantage.

Body Signals to Look for in a Negotiation

In addition to covering up your real intentions through your body language, you observe your opponent's nonverbal cues to enhance your negotiation efforts. For better negotiation results, observe your opponent. Here are some of the things you have to look out for when observing the other party.

Creases at the Forehead

Apparent creases (unnatural wrinkles) on the forehead is a sign of stress and the absence of these creases means that the person is calm and going easy during negotiations.

Eyes

It is important to observe the direction of the eyes of the other negotiator to assess information. Eyes opened wide indicate interest and attentiveness while being open-minded. On the contrary, narrowing of the eyes signals a higher degree of focus on the subject.

To gain an accurate assessment of their eye movements, you first need to establish a baseline. Do this while in a non-threatening environment prior to the official negotiation. To establish a baseline, you should ask questions pertaining to an everyday situation like:

- How is the weather today?
- How long have you been in this business?
- Do you like watching sports?

Ask questions that may allow the other person to think about their answers so you can observe eye movements—Is the movement towards the left, or right?

Is the person looking upward or downward? Follow up with other non-threatening questions to confirm how the person's eyes move when trying to recall something.

Speech Pace

Another aspect that you need to closely observe in the other person is their speech pace. How fast or how slow is the person speaking? Generally, people's normal pace is between 110-150 words per minute. As a person gets more excited, this can increase to 175-240 words per minute. This rate also suggests anxiety or discomfort.

To be able to gain insight into the mental perspective of your counterpart to the negotiation, observe the point where his speech tends to quicken and why it occurs at that specific point? Also take note of any moisture on his lips, hands, or brows. These indicate nervousness or anxiety when there is a quickening of speech. Knowing all these can make you maneuver the person either into a heightened state of agitation or calmness, whichever suits your objective at the time of the negotiation.

Hand Movements

It helps a great deal to observe the body language of someone you are negotiating with especially the movements of the hands. You should learn to observe their hands as hands convey a lot of hidden information in a negotiation.

For example, people use their hands to show appreciation by clapping. Others display their hands to show displeasure. Even while speaking, hand movements give insight into thoughts being processed. So, when someone is speaking, the movement of their hands add or detract the message they are trying to deliver. The same is true when you are conveying information.

Sometimes, you can observe that there's a difference in a person's body language and with their words. If this happens, you have to pay more attention to nonverbal communication. Body language discloses a person's intent more than their words.

Open hand gestures signify that the person is not fearful but when hands are closed like rubbing together or rubbing other parts of the body or getting close to the body, it shows that the person is anxious or too cautious. When you want to make a good impression, keep hands open and avoid making gestures that might be seen as indecisive or not in consonance with your words. Doing so will likely reduce your ability to persuade.

Here are some hands movements that you should lightly consider when conversing with someone but strongly consider when negotiating.

Hand Close to the Body

If the person you are dealing with is guarding their thoughts, you are more likely to find their hands closer to the body. This happens when that person senses threats to their well-being. Their hands are positioned to protect themselves from perceived indifference.

When you see this at the start of any negotiation, it helps to put the other person at ease. You may have to address a point that made the other person uncomfortable before you can induce a positive atmosphere conducive to a winning negotiation.

Hands With Fingers Interlocked

A negotiation displaying hands with interlocking fingers suggests that they are not open to your suggestion, offer or counteroffer.

Once you have obtained the pattern in their eye movements related to when they are recalling information, you will be able to determine if the person is lying or being truthful during the actual negotiation.

To confirm your observation, notice certain acts like having hands with interlocked fingers as this usually implies not being receptive to your offer during negotiations. Take note of the response given. If the person unlocked their fingers, ask them to proceed. In this situation, you have made some changes to their body language and made the person more mentally receptive to you and your offer. Another thing, you have given the person the lead and therefore will highlight what they consider important.

Hands Pushed Away With Palms Out

Take note of this gesture as it implies that the person has no interest in what is being offered. You can, likewise, measure the level of disagreement by the way the palms are pushed outward. You must also be aware of when the other person voices their assertions that are in agreeance with you. Is this case, their body language contradicts real feelings, so believe the gestures more than the words.

Feet

Both feet of parties involved in a negotiation must be facing each other. When one person turns a foot away, it means that a person has disengaged from negotiations and will soon leave.

Touching

The degree of touching between negotiators depends on how they are familiar with each other. Therefore, it is crucial that you are mindful of how you touch the other person. You may not want to be perceived negatively. Take note of how the person reacts when touched. Were they slightly pulling back or flinching? That's a sure sign that you have overstepped the boundary. Pay close attention so you can gauge how you are being received.

Voice and Tone

Be sensitive to the other person's tone especially when there are any changes that occur while negotiating. Ending a sentence with a high pitch can turn a statement into a question. This can make you sound less in authority than what you actually intended.

All of this body language or nonverbal cues can have an impact on how your words can be perceived by the other party. So be mindful of how you deliver your body language more than your words.

Signs that You Have the Other Person's Full Attention

There are signs that indicate the person is listening and absorbing everything that you are saying, which will most likely end things in your favor.

Hands on the Cheek

This gesture signifies genuine interest and that a person is evaluating things in their mind while listening to your offer. It is, therefore, useful to ask questions or solicit ideas to hear thoughts.

Chin Stroking

It is at this point when the other party could be making a decision, so try not to interrupt! Look out instead for the next cue as when the person leans back and crosses their arms. These are negative gestures which mean a big NO!

Draw points of agreement and clarify any disagreement. However, if the person leans forward, keep silent and allow them to talk.

Seated Readiness

This indicates excitement and agreement. If followed by stroking of the chin, it's as good as saying YES! At this point, use the word "we" to point out that you're both in agreement.

Head Tilted

When the head is tilted, it means the person is showing interest in whatever it is you're offering. You may use these gestures to show interest and create a perception of being a good listener.

Tell-Tale Signs of Disagreement

There are negative nonverbal signs to show that the person disagrees with you or is simply hostile. It's best to read the person's gestures in a cluster than read a single cue to avoid misreading the message conveyed by their body language.

Crossed Arms

Generally, this move is an indication of being defensive. It doesn't mean that the person simply shut themselves off from any discussion or listening to any of it. It's just a matter of filtering everything being heard that affects the other person. According to Gerald I Nierenberger who wrote the book, *How to Read a Person Like A Book,* in a study involving more than 2000 negotiations, not one was closed when negotiating participants had arms and legs crossed during the negotiation. For those with participants who have negotiators with opened arms and legs, they were able to reach a deal.

Hand Supporting the Chin

This gesture implies boredom and has no interest whatsoever on what is being discussed. When this gesture is combined with vacant nods and glazed eyes, it means you indeed have lost connection with your audience. It could be that your speech is too long it, your audience is bored, or you're giving to many details that simply didn't interest your listener. Try to be direct in your negotiation. Remember that businesspeople have little time to spare and most of the time, their minds are busy somewhere else, so you need to prove yourself interesting.

To test if the person is still with you, stop talking. This can make the other person jump in and move on to something else. Sometimes, boredom can be a result of your talking more about yourself than the deal itself.

Chapter 11: Is Faking Body Language Possible?

Can you learn body language and acquire it as a skill?

Can you fake your body language?

It is possible for you to learn the common body language but according to new studies, there is a whole new set of cues that, if not possible, could be difficult to control.

Through being conscious and careful repetition, one can be more confident and easily learn some of this body language:

- Keep your hands out of your pockets.
- To remain open and honest, use your hands expressively.
- Keep your hands away from your face.

Microexpressions

Microexpressions are simple facial expressions that may happen in a split second and momentarily reveal your emotions. Microexpressions or micro signals are helpful so that you may be able to discern a liar from an honest person. These may range from a frown, furrow, wrinkles, smirk, or a smile. These serve as a fleeting glimpse into a person's inner feelings.

The frontalis, risorius and corrugator muscles are responsible for the appearance of microexpressions. They are stimulated by your emotions and almost impossible to control consciously. Let's take the fake smile as an example. A fake smile is an expression that we use in order to show someone that we are happy even if we really are not. Fake smiles are easily detected when given attention because though the lip muscles are pulled across your mouth to form a smile, the muscles controlling the eyes do not go together and play their part.

Researchers use specialized computer software to detect micro signals. They use computers so they can catch the fleeting facial expression that happens so fast that it is almost impossible for another human to pick up consciously.

High-speed cameras may also be used. By slowing down videos, repeating and observing them carefully, you may be able to detect microexpressions.

It may be difficult to detect and control microexpressions but the fact is, at some levels, the ability to detect and understand them has evolved. You must not underestimate microexpressions because it can simply betray your inward emotions in a blink of an eye and can be detected by good observers. Never assume that you can easily fake your way in conversations or even without speaking because these minute actions say a lot about your true emotions.

You might notice times when you meet a person and have a feeling that that person can't be trusted. It may be that your subconscious intuition is at work and gives you the feeling of mistrust towards that person that you couldn't formulate into words. The reason behind that is the combination of your intuition and micro-signals that you picked up from the person.

You might encounter researchers who say that the part of the body easiest to control is the face. This is not absolutely true as you can find circumstances in which the result is contrary to that statement.

A good example of that is the botox treatment in which the facial muscles are injected with low-level toxins so as to avoid wrinkles from appearing. If facial muscles are the easiest to control, why can't we just avoid using these muscles so that we won't have wrinkles when we age? It's because it's not that just as simple as we think. If the majority of our muscles are under our deliberate control, we'll just focus on controlling these muscles and we'll not be able to focus on other things that are of more importance.

Another example is about speech control. Notice whenever we speak there are appropriate gestures and facial expressions that go along with it. Did you ever try expressing your deepest feelings with other people but at the same time, you are controlling your face muscles contrary to the feeling that you need to portray? Or you remain poker-faced despite overflowing emotions while you speak out? Facial expressions are our natural response to whatever is happening around us. It is closely connected to our emotions and thoughts. It enables us to identify the precise feelings of the portrayer and that's why we rely on reading it most of the time.

Another way to detect insincerity is through observing incongruent body language. It means that what you say is inconsistent with what you are doing. Women are experts in this area because they have the ability to perceive the whole picture and can identify obscurities and artifices in persons and circumstances faster than men. Also, according to some researches, women can perform multiple tasks at once.

Oftentimes, you will hear women say their senses tingle when they feel that something isn't right (female intuition). The good thing is that men can also develop this skill through practice.

Chapter 12: Training Exercises to Improve Body Language

Your body language—your posture, gestures, position, and facial expressions—affects the people around you and even your own emotions. This works vice versa; that is, their body language also influences yours.

Whether we like or not, emotions motivate all of us. One of the best ways to enhance that drive is to improve your body language. Sooner or later, the change that started from you will reverberate to those around you, resulting in an overall change in your environment.

Most of us can't directly change our emotions but we can definitely change our body language in order to upgrade our lifestyle. This chapter introduces training exercising that would help enhance your nonverbal behavior.

Body Language Exercises (Solo)

This simple exercise is intended for you to get know your own nonverbal behavior including your facial expressions and body language.

Instructions

- Talk, walk and act in front of your mirror (preferably a full-length mirror).
- Take a candid video of yourself then review it. Give appropriate feedback regarding your body language in a given situation.
- Pick up a good habit (e.g. observing proper posture) or unlearn a bad one (e.g. pointing your finger at someone or putting your hands inside your pockets). Consistently practice this new habit until it becomes imprinted in you.
- Ask a close friend or your family to observe you and pinpoint the body language you need to work on in order to improve.

Many individuals find public speaking intimidating. They feel nervous to be exposed to a lot of people and vulnerable to criticism in the process. Simply put, they lack the confidence to face others. However, research shows that you can trick your emotions using your own body language. For instance, you can convince yourself that you feel happy when you keep on smiling. This is the same as the feeling of confidence during public speaking. Improving your posture, gestures, and facial expressions will help you confidently face and speak even to a myriad of people.

For this exercise, it would help to practice in a vacant, open-spaced area or you can start doing this at home. This is also to be carried out several days (or weeks if you must) before your public speaking engagement.

Instructions

- Think of the most common facial expressions, gestures, and body language associated with positive emotions.
- Stand in the vacant area and visualize a setting wherein you are standing before the members of the board, students, or a VIP.
- Relax your body, distributing your weight on both your feet. As you do this, think of these assertions in order to positively condition your mind: I feel great. I am cool. I can do this. I am the best!
- Square your shoulders, straighten your back, relax your arms at your sides, and begin to confidently walk forward as you recite your mantra with confidence. If it helps, you can speak the mantra out loud. Once you've reached the other end of the

area (or your room), turn around and continue to walk with the same attitude. Continue to practice this every day.

- Bring the challenge up to another level by going to a busy part of the town and walking the way you have been practicing (without reciting the mantra out loud, of course). Repeat this confidence exercise and don't be afraid to grab various opportunities when you can show the results of this exercise.

Your body language tells a lot of things about you. When it speaks confidence and reliability, many people would be drawn to you and as they say, people always introduce opportunities. This exercise aims to help you develop the body language of a leader.

Instructions

- Begin with your posture. People's attention is often drawn by someone with good posture—whether standing, walking or sitting. Posture often reflects your inner state of mind. People with a positive outlook in life often carry themselves with confidence, that is with the back straight and chest out. Always check yourself to see if you are stooping or slouching.

- Release your tension and inhibitions. Get rid of the tension in your neck, shoulder, jaw, and tongue by putting two fingertips in your mouth right under your tongue then slowly releasing them. Remember, your tongue should be relaxed during the process. It shouldn't appear concave, convex or too tensed. Put your other hand under your lip line, creating a V between your index finger and thumb. Gently pull your jaw down to about half to one inch. Observe yourself in the mirror and see how your tongue might pull back or your neck and shoulders become tense. Do this exercise regularly and you will feel more relaxed and confident over time.
- Make sure that your gestures are purposeful. Gestures put power and emphasis on your message so it's advisable not to overuse them. They shouldn't just be random, repetitive or unintentional. You can practice them as you speak in front of the mirror. Observe how each gesture visually intensifies or abates a word or a sentence in your speech.
- Work on your handshake since it is the first connection you make with another person. In the eyes of the third party, it may look like a simple

greeting gesture, but it actually says a lot. A handshake serves as an equalizer and tells the sincerity and warmth of a person. A lousy and fleeting handshake or an aggressive one puts you in a disadvantage. On the other hand, a firm and sincere handshake helps establish trust. Maintain eye contact while shaking hands and never rush.

Body Language Exercises (Group Activity)

This exercise helps illustrate relevant points on body language. The participants are trained to readily understand a particular mood based on the given nonverbal signals of a person. By identifying the signals, specifically the negative ones, the emotional contagion can be avoided. This is particularly helpful in the workplace where people are expected to improve their relationships by controlling and improving their body language.

Objective

To be aware of the different nonverbal signals and identify the mood behind them.

Needed Materials

"Emotion cards" with the following emotions depicted on them:

- Satisfied
- Bored
- Frustrated
- Impressed
- Traumatized
- Depressed
- Happy
- Confident
- Angry
- Nervous
- Stressed
- Cynical
- Agitated
- Unconvinced
- Peaceful
- Scared
- Surprised
- Disgusted

Timing

Explaining the exercise: 2 minutes

Activity: 10 minutes

Discussion: 5-10 minutes

Instructions

- The facilitator should ask for a volunteer who will enact the emotion stated on the given emotion card.
- The participants should sit at one side of the room. The volunteer will then stand in front of the participants and proceed to act out what was written in the card.
- The participants should guess the emotion and proceed to discuss the body language used to portray it.
- Repeat the process until everybody has been given the chance to perform in front.

Questions for the Group Discussion

- How easy was it to enact and give the corresponding body language based on the emotions in the emotion card?
- How would you feel when confronted by the person with negative emotions such as anger, fear, disgust, etc.?
- Were there times when you felt your own mood changed based on the (negative or positive) body

language exhibited by a certain person in your workplace or at home?
- When someone was depressed or stressed out, did you feel the same way, too?
- How can you control your own emotions or negative nonverbal behavior in order to avoid affecting other people?

Objective

Identify nonverbal cues and explain the meaning behind these signals by observing the people in various situations as portrayed in the images or videos.

Needed Materials

Set of images or video clips showing various people in daily situations based on these ideas:

- People during a board meeting
- A teacher during his or her class
- Two individuals greeting each other
- People while waiting in a subway station, airport, etc.
- A politician during an interview or press conference
- An individual during a public plea regarding a missing family member or relative

Timing

Explaining the exercise: 2 minutes

Activity: 10-20 minutes

Discussion: 5-10 minutes

Instructions

- Each participant should be able to take notes based on what they see or observe in each image or video presentation, paying closer attention to facial expressions, body language, posture, and other nonverbal behavior.
- Each participant should be able to share their notes.
- Encourage discussion based on the participants' different opinions.
- Questions for the group discussion.
- How easy was it to understand and interpret nonverbal communication?
- Was there a pattern in common postures, gestures or tone of voice for a particular emotion?
- Do you think the people in the images or videos were conscious about their body language during that certain time?

- What is the importance of understanding body language?
- Which areas should you focus on learning the most?

Some people are really fast talkers, talking at the same pace as we think. Because of this, they can't help but to mumble short sentences and skip words, making what they say sound incoherent. Although they are smart, others think that they're quite the opposite.

This exercise is designed for fast talkers to help them improve their diction and gain confidence by eloquently expressing themselves.

Objective

Help participants to talk at an ideal speed and also allow them to express what they're saying using various gestures and nonverbal cues.

Time

Explaining the exercise: 5 minutes

Activity: 20 minutes (10 minutes per round)

Group Discussion: 10 minutes

Instructions

- Working in pairs, the participants should choose who will be the talker and the imitator. Talkers will be those who are going to choose a subject they will talk about. They can talk about everything like their experience in their previous vacation, everyday work experience, a Caribbean adventure, their high school adventure or about a story they read about.
- While the talkers tell about their stories, the imitators will act out what they hear using various gestures and body language. This method helps both parties in two important areas: First, the talkers are forced to talk at a slower pace so that the imitators will have the time to understand and enact what they say. Secondly, the imitators are forced to concentrate on what the talkers have to tell so they can express it accordingly.
- After ten minutes, the partners should switch roles and perform the exercise for another ten minutes.
- Gather everyone for a group discussion.

Questions for the Group Discussion

- How can you assess your talking speed? Did the exercise help you slow it down?

- Do you think you can adjust your speed next time even without your imitator?

The exercise aims to help you identify various nonverbal cues and realize how these signals affect the way you communicate with other people. You get trained on how to understand the importance of communication in a given social context without using words. Moreover, this exercise helps you enhance your writing creativity.

Objective

Write a short story that should be carried out using body language.

Needed Materials

- Pen
- Paper

Time

Explaining the exercise: 5 minutes

Creating the dialogue: 30 minutes

Performance: 5 minutes per group

Group Discussion: 10 minutes

Instructions

- Working in pairs, discuss and write down a 600-word dialogue within 30 minutes. Make sure that each line can be acted out using gestures, facial expressions, and body language.
- The narrator (the facilitator) will then read the story or dialogue and the pair of actors will proceed to act out their lines using body language.
- The audience (those who are not yet performing) should be able to provide feedback after each story.
- After every pair is finished, call for a group discussion.

Questions for the Group Discussion

- What was your first impression when you were asked to create a story/ dialogue? Did you think that it's going to be challenging?
- Did you find writing the story/ dialogue hard? What's the difficulty of the task?
- How did you find acting or communicating through body language? Was it easy or difficult?
- How does this exercise improve your nonverbal expressions?

Objective

Write a story or dialogue, design characters, and act it out.

Needed Materials

- Time Pen
- Paper (A4)

Time

- Explaining the exercise: 5 minutes
- Part 1 Writing and planning activity: 20 minutes
- Part 2 Writing and planning activity: 20 minutes
- Part 3 Presentation: (role play discussion) 10 minutes and (actual presentation) 5 minutes per group
- Post Presentation Feedback: 5 minutes after each presentation
- Group Discussion: 10 minutes

Instructions

Part 1

The participants should be divided into three groups. Ask each group to design two characters. They can get ideas from the people they know or get inspiration from characters in popular movies, TV series, or novels.

The participants should write their character sketches in an A4-sized paper using a narrative description. Each sketch should tell who the character is without having it say or do anything (Note: Each character sketch should not exceed one A4-sized paper.) Work on the sketch for 20 minutes.

Part 2

Each group should pass their character sketch to the group on their left. This time, each group should take time to study and understand the character sketches they received. They are discouraged to discuss the sketches with the original group who made the sketch or with other groups.

The groups should use the characters in a scenario or a story. They should write a dramatic dialogue between the two characters. In the scene, each character should have a secret they cannot divulge with each other, not even to the audience (Note: The dialogue should not exceed two A4-sized papers.) Work on the dialogue for 20 minutes.

Part 3

The groups should pass the dialogue they made (but not the character sketches) to the group on their left. They need to review and understand the dialogue and select two of their members to act out the story in front of the whole class. Allow 10 minutes for them to talk about their plans for the role play.

Each group should present their skit for about 5 minutes per presentation. The actors should be able to effectively express their characters using various gestures, facial expressions, and body language.

After each presentation, the viewers are allowed to give comments on the character design, dialogues, and the actual presentation.

Proceed with the general discussion after the presentations.

Questions for the Group Discussion

- What are your opinions about the process of designing the characters?
- What can you say about the process of creating the dialogues based on the character sketches?
- (To the actors) How do you find the process of acting out the characters based on the dialogues?
- What gestures, facial expressions, or body language are used to support or define the given traits of each character in the story?

This exercise helps the participants to understand and recognize the power of making eye contact as it can affect emotional connection and relationship between people, particularly in the work setting.

Objective

Establish the habit of making eye contact, thus, helping the participants develop positive body language

Needed Materials

- Blank cards or index cards for easy writing while standing
- Pen

Timing

Explaining the exercise: 5 minutes

Activity (Stages 1-2): 5 minutes

Group Discussion: 10 minutes

Instructions

Stage 1

The participants should freely roam the room like they were in the public place and they don't know each other.

They are not yet encouraged to establish eye contact this time. Do this for about a minute.

After the allotted time, ask them to stop and write down how they felt during that time.

Stage 2

The participants should try making eye contact with each other as they go about the room but they should immediately break it and look away. Allow this for two minutes.

Again, stop everyone and let them write down how they felt during those two minutes.

Stage 3

For this round, ask the participants to establish eye contact and as soon as they do this, they should pair up together. They should stand together at a particular spot in the room, refusing to make eye contact with the rest of the group for two minutes.

After two minutes, the participants should write down how they felt.

End this activity and call for a group discussion.

Questions for the Group Discussion

- How did you feel during the various stages of the activity?
- How did you feel when you didn't have to make eye contact with the people around you?
- How did you feel when you needed to break the eye contact right away?
- How did you feel when you established eye contact and had to pair up with your partner?
- Did you immediately find someone you could pair up with? If not, how did you feel about it?
- What kind of preconditioning triggers our behavior in trying to make eye contact and maintaining it?
- How does this simple practice differ in various societies all around the globe? Cite different examples of this.

Conclusion

Acquiring skills related to understanding, reading, and analyzing nonverbal communication or body language can be useful in itself. It's a handy tool that gives you the edge over others as you can use it to improve all aspects of your life – personal, relationships, career, and business.

Mastering this skill can help you communicate and understand other people and the messages they want to convey other than the use of words. It can be a lot of fun knowing what other people are thinking, especially when they are lying, and how comfortable they are in a given situation.

That said, the nonverbal cues we are trying to interpret are not going to tell us 100 percent what the other person is feeling or thinking. However, once you find clues that will help you understand other people better, you can use them to communicate effectively as you gain more awareness of those around you. All you need to do is pay more attention to people's actions, movements, and reactions as you, likewise, become more sensitive to your natural human intuition blended with logic and reason.

Book - II

Dark Psychology Secrets

Learn Usage and Defense Techniques of Manipulation, Persuasion, Emotional Influence, Mind Control, and Covert NLP

Introduction

Dark Psychology has been around forever. You can bet that it's been used on you and you've used it on others – whether you were aware of that or not.

Politicians are avid users of this type of manipulation. Cult leaders also use dark psychology to gain followers then they delve further into the manipulations to get their followers to do as they want them too. This includes handing the leader all their belongings and money - all the way to committing crimes for them.

Not everyone is susceptible to these kinds of manipulations. But those who are at risk for being used by people who know how to use this dark art, rarely know that fact about themselves.

Understanding yourself and what you will and won't fall for is essential in protecting yourself from these users. And if you're reading this so that you can learn to use this form of manipulation, then you will understand how to spot those people who are easier to pull into your web. Of course, I hope that's not the case as those who seek to hurt others have to face karmic justice, and that's never any fun.

Being that dark psychology is so abundant, it's never been more important to understand it completely. There are many things you can do to combat this evil. There are many ways to see through those people who seek to fool you, lull you into a sense of security, then snatch your sanity away from you.

We're catching it from all sides – political, spiritual, religious, and even from those you think you can trust, like family members and love interests. Once you fully understand what's out there and how you can notice it, defend yourself against it, or just walk away from it, you will find yourself feeling better about yourself and life in general.

Don't think for a second that the tactics used in dark psychology can't injure people. The scars that are left from being the victim of a hateful manipulator run as deep as those left from physical trauma. Sometimes these scars are even worse than physical ones that others can see and understand.

Some people even do their research on how to get people to do what they want. Some strive to not only pull the wool over people's eyes but to manipulate them in hurtful ways as well. Things aren't always so open, so black and white. There's plenty of grey areas too. In those areas is where deceit lies. In those areas is where danger hides.

Understanding dark psychology is a thing everyone should be able to do. Guarding yourself against the onslaught of psychological warfare is of the utmost importance.

If you don't read this for yourself, then do it for those you love. Learn how to spot those who seek to destroy others. Learn how to deal with them effectively.

Like bullies, manipulators don't keep trying to manipulate someone who sees through them. They won't waste any more time on you, once you can see them for who and what they are. They'll move on to the next victim, but at least your time under their dark spell will be over, and you can begin to recover from their attacks.

So, prepare yourself to be enlightened in a way you've never been before as light is about to be shed on the darkness of the psychology used by manipulators and evildoers all over the world.

Chapter 1: What is Dark Psychology

One must not fool themselves into thinking they've never had a devious thought in their lives. As humans – like animals – because we are animals – every single one of us has it within ourselves to do harm to others. Survival of the fittest is a thing we're born with. This type of instinct is natural and even necessary if we're to live fruitful lives.

Hurting someone who is hurting you or someone you love is instinctive. Even killing someone to save yourself or another creature – be it human or animal- is understandable and instinctive.

What isn't instinctive is hurting another creature just to hurt it. There's a lot of power in knowing you can cause someone pain with only your words and actions alone. While most see that power and refuse to abuse it, others see the power and exploit it.

Dark Psychology is a science. The study of insidious behavior, manipulative practices, and anything used to hurt people without any reason or remorse are considered Dark Psychology.

Dark manipulators have always been around. If your belief system is in the Bible, then you've heard how the serpent manipulated Eve into taking a bite of the forbidden apple – this practice is that ancient – *the beginning of humanity, ancient.*

No matter what beliefs you have about how life on our planet began, you know history is full of people who hurt others - just to do it. You know that millions upon millions of innocent people have died at the hands of people who have used the dark art to make others believe the same evil way that they did. The holocaust would have never occurred had there not been the dark mind of one man who manipulated so many other people to do his horrific bidding. What's worse is that he wasn't the only person to do something that evil. More rulers did the same thing before he was ever born.

What makes people want to harm others, both physically and mentally?

Perhaps their childhood was torturous. Perhaps they were born with a mental impairment that science has yet to uncover. Whatever the reasons are make no difference. There are people with dark intentions – end of story.

People who study Dark Psychology are looking for answers as to why human beings would do such evil things. What made them decide to hurt others? What makes them think the way they do? Why would they seek to control others? And why do they pick the people to manipulate that they do?

Dark psychologists believe that all humans are born with a dark side. Some can control it better than others is the theory. But why can some control it and others can't — or don't want to?

Dark Singularity is a term that means there is a part of the human psyche that allows a person to commit immoral acts without any purpose or remorse for what they've done. Most people who commit crimes against others have some reason behind it — something they can blame their actions on. True dark souls blame their actions on others or merely refuse to self-reflect to let anyone know why they did what they did.

With internet access, the darkness has never been easier to spread. You've got to watch out for these people in your everyday life and on the internet as well. The way these dark people can spread misery is nearly limitless. They can destroy your credit — your credibility — your relationships, and more.

Using their dark thoughts to come up with things they can do to hurt others, people can now take over a person's identity. Your banking accounts are fair game – and they don't have to get a gun to rob banks anymore either. They can even steal your heart online now. Catfishing is a thing that's become somewhat commonplace on the internet now. Even your heart's not safe anymore – if you decide to believe some of these masterminds.

Most who do this online scamming can't even be caught. If they are, sometimes it's hard for authorities to define the jurisdiction of the crime. Most of these people get off scot-free. But their victims are left hurt, confused, and bitter. When even the systems you thought could help you - can't, then you're left wondering what happened to the justice in this world.

Deception is practiced online in a way that wasn't even imaginable a decade ago. Lies can go viral in a matter of minutes now. It's so bad that the news media has had to come up with fact-checkers to weed through the lies and fake news to get to what's real. We live in dark times, always having to second-guess things we hear and read and sometimes even see firsthand.

Defamation of character used to be pretty hard to do. One would have to talk to a lot of different people to spread so many lies about one person that it would destroy their reputation – worldwide. That can be done in minutes now.

Understanding certain things about the people you interact with, both in person and online, has never been more important. You can't let your guard down even for a moment when dealing with new people in your life. If you do, then you might be letting the devil himself into your midst. At least that's how it'll feel when you're going through things you couldn't even imagine before they came along.

Psychologists and criminologists have set some standards to measure darkness in people. There are varying degrees of these dark traits. Three mental disorders have helped psychologists catalogue a number of characteristics. The Dark Triad consists of three sets of behavior – narcissism, psychopathy, and Machiavellianism. The most frightening thing about being exposed to people with any of – or worse – all these conditions – is that it can be detrimental to *your* mental wellbeing. You can literally be driven crazy by these people.

The traits to look for in a person aren't always easy to spot. Manipulation, exploitation, and lack of remorse are significant parts of all three disorders in the Dark Triad. While narcissists need admiration, control, and to be the center of attention – as the world revolves around them in their minds, that's not true of people with the other dark traits.

Psychopaths can be charming, brilliant, and more physically dangerous than people would ever expect them to be. The same can be said for

Machiavellians, while narcissists tend to hurt themselves physically.

Narcissists harm themselves to get attention, pity, and martyr themselves. They love to play the victim, even when it's you who is really hurting – especially when they lie to get people to think you did something to hurt them, making you look bad.

Lies are prevalent with all members of the dark triad. Watching out for those who tend to lie about things when the truth would do just fine is step one in protecting yourself against those who seek to do you harm. And don't think you're tough enough not to get hurt by anyone who has any of these disorders. The way they slip into your head makes it nearly impossible to understand what they're doing until it's too late.

If you've been raised by a person with any of these conditions, things might not look the same way to you that they do to others. If a narcissist raised you, you might have low self-esteem. You might believe that you're just not good enough for certain things or people. The love you experienced from that narcissistic parent was conditional. You had to earn their approval and time and time again were told you hadn't accomplished that task.

Being the child of a narcissist isn't easy. It's never about you – even when it's supposed to be. It might be your birthday. The day is all about you, right? Wrong.

Let's say it was your mother, who was the narcissist in this situation. You would hear her complaining quietly to others how hard she worked to get the party together. She had to make the cake, the decorations, the invitations. She had to clean the house, set up the extra tables, and invite people over she doesn't even like – her in-laws. Her back went out while moving furniture around to accommodate everyone – she's been suffering in silence for days. Only she hasn't been silent at all. She's been whimpering, moaning, drawing attention to her pain but when asked only says it's nothing, she'll be fine, she's a trooper after all.

How can you enjoy your birthday, knowing that your mother has gone through such hardships just for you?

The answer is, you can't. And your mother's reward is seeing your eyes downcast, your shoulders slumped, and an apology on your lips for even wanting a party for your birthday. She's done what she intended to do all along – she's ruined it for you.

Giving you things, then putting a penalty on it is just one of the dirty tricks that narcissists play on their victims. Whether these people are aware of what they're doing or not, it still ends up damaging the people in their lives.

If being raised by a narcissist sounds terrible, think about being raised by a psychopath. In most cases, it's the female psychopath who is raising the child. Psychopaths, in general, are selfish and that means most men who are psychopathic won't stick around to raise their offspring anyway – thus the mother psychopath scenario.

Lacking empathy, the psychopathic mother can't forge the bond with her children that come out naturally to mothers without this disorder. She's not as engaged with the baby from the beginning – even during the pregnancy. Neglect is prominent when others aren't around to witness it. She'll leave the child or children to themselves most of the time. When other people are around though, she's completely different. She's on top of things – the super-mom who does it all for her kids.

In the child's eyes, nothing makes much sense. Mom's all about us? Does mom live her life for us? But she doesn't even make dinner for us most nights unless she's hungry.

When she does pay attention to her kids, it's only to mold them into what she needs them to be. One day, she'll turn to prey on them after all. She'll exploit them, use them for money and whatever else she needs.

People who've been raised by a psychopath have self-doubt, confusion, and even guilt. With more mental scars than most, they're fragile in ways others can't comprehend. Some may seem to have strengths most don't, but that's only because they had to be something a child should never have to be - the protector and caregiver for their siblings and themselves. While looking strong on the outside, they're weak as kittens on the inside and straddle the bar mentally, often thinking one day they too will fall over into the insanity they knew their mother lived in.

On to being raised by a Machiavellian. It's important to know what traits a Machiavellian has. They focus on themselves, value power and money over everything else, and lie when they feel it will work for them. With a lack of empathy, it makes it easy for them to commit acts that harm others without feeling any remorse for it. They have the patience it takes to deviously calculate a plan and to see it through to fruition.

What does this mean for the child of someone who has this personality disorder?

Bad things.

In a Machiavellian's parenting skillset, there are things utilized that most parents deem immoral and even plain mean. Pitting siblings against each other in an attempt to get the most out of each of them is one of their tactics. Picture little Susie and her older brother Bobby in a contest to see who can make the best math grade for the semester. Picture the afflicted parent throwing in some choice words, 'You mean to tell me that your little sister did better than you did, Bobby? You must be so embarrassed. You must feel like a total loser.'

Since lying is a thing they believe is perfectly acceptable when the ends justify the means, the Machiavellian's use of it only serves to show their children that lying is okay to do. It also teaches them that people lie, and no one can really be trusted on their word. As you can imagine, this means the child of a person with this disorder sees others as liars and manipulators as well and treats them as such. This makes life hard.

Discipline is also very harsh. Expectations are high. Not meeting the high expectations results in punishment and embarrassment. In these families, it's essential that every individual is viewed as perfect from the outside world's perspective. You *must* make the best grades. You *must* be the most well-behaved children in public as well as at home. You need to maintain your physical appearance at all times, being sure to stay well-groomed and attractive. Everything about the Machiavellian's family must not only seem perfect; it must *be* perfect.

For those who've been raised by a person who has all three of these personality disorders, it's a nightmare. Much like being raised by someone with multiple personalities, the child of someone with all these disorders never knows which one of the ugly heads will be raised against them at any given time. It takes a toll on a person to be raised by such a parent.

In Dark Psychology, subjects don't always have every disorder; some only have certain traits. Some of these traits can be used to manipulate people. This is why some people seek knowledge about the characteristics of people with these three disorders. Some people want to understand how to use these tactics to get what they want.

Others want to understand these tactics to arm themselves against those who seek to use these psychological weapons against them. And still, others only want to understand these traits because they grew up under parents who had them.

Whatever your reason is for wanting to know more about Dark Psychology, remember that harming others is morally wrong. If you've been hurt by someone who used these dark manipulations on you, you might think about seeking counseling to help you heal the wounds they've left. While knowing can help you to understand why you feel and do the things you do, therapy will help you move on with your life in a healthier way.

Perhaps you've suspected yourself of having one or all of these disorders or at least some characteristics of them. You too can get help if you seek counseling. There's no shame in admitting that you need help to overcome something. We all have darkness in us. We all have immoral thoughts. Most of us would never think we'd act on. Maybe you've acted on some of your dark thoughts. It doesn't make you a monster. It just means you might need some help to do better in life – live morally and not hurt others anymore.

In the following pages, you will learn things you most likely never knew before. With this knowledge comes the responsibility to use what you learn wisely and not for evil intent.

Do unto others as you would have them do unto you.

Chapter 2 : Are You at Risk for Manipulation

Let's face it; people can only get away with manipulations because so many of us fall for them. It's become a lucrative business, marketing to trusting people who will believe whatever is dished out to them. All one must do is open a magazine or a webpage to find ads for all sorts of things. Things that promise you wrinkle-free skin, pills that can actually make you smarter, and the top ten ways to make a million bucks before your twenty-first birthday.

These promotional marketing campaigns all have one thing in common; they're preying on people with similar characteristics. These same characteristics are the ones that dark manipulators look for in a person.

Of course, you've got your Dark Triad to watch out for, but you've got all kinds of people with some of the characteristics to watch out for too.

You've got to remember that everyone has access to the same knowledge you do. And not all of them use it for good purposes.

The things manipulators are looking for in a victim might surprise you. You might be tested by someone asking you if you caught the news last night, "Did you see the report on contaminated broccoli?"

Maybe you missed that one. "No. What happened?"

Keen to learn if you're the type of person to fall for things easily, the manipulator tests the waters before diving all the way in with the lie, "It's killing people all over the Southwestern United States. I'm kind of surprised you haven't heard about it."

"Killing people? And this was on the news, right? Not some social media bologna, right?"

"Right there on the six o'clock news last night."

Visibly shaken, you recall eating broccoli only last week. "How long did it take for symptoms to show up, do you know?"

That's all the manipulator needs to know. It's pretty obvious you're one of those people – *an easy target.*

Do you watch the news and believe most of it, without thinking anything else about it? Maybe some of the reports seemed a little too dramatic, but that's the world we live in nowadays. And maybe you're just too trusting in humanity.

Do you tend to act like a child – think things are unfair?

If you do, then you're making yourself easy for someone to manipulate if they know this about you. All they have to do is speak to that inner child who resides way too close to the surface in you, and they'll have you eating out of the palm of their hands in no time.

Do you listen intently in church and bring home with you a mantra the preacher used a lot? Did you do your research to make sure this mantra was true? If not, you might be allowing yourself to fall into a way of thinking that you might not do on your own. You might be easily led down the wrong path by someone with bad intentions.

Are you one of those people who think they can find a shortcut while others are suckers for going a long way around? Maybe you'd like to shed some unwanted pounds but going to the gym and eating healthy sound like a drag to you. You've heard about this miracle pill that claims to melt the fat off you like butter off a hot knife. You'll try that instead of eating veggies and sweating to the oldies. And maybe you'd fall for some other bull too if the right person puts it in front of you and tells you that it's a shortcut.

Does the uncertain scare you? Would you rather deal with things the way they are now and always have been instead of trying something new? Would you rather do this because you're afraid of trying something new? Do you often make excuses for why you stick to the old and outdated when something better is out there? If so, then you might make an easy mark for the right predator.

Trying new things is smart. Easier and better things happen all the time and why get left behind just because you're afraid of change? When you get left behind, you'll find yourself alone. That's when the real danger can drift in.

What resonates with you more – getting what you want now and not thinking about how that might affect you in the long-run or making sure you take your time to make big decisions that could affect the rest of your life?

If you care more about the right now, instead of the long-term, you could get taken advantage of easily. Some slick talker could get you into a financial bind or sell you some piece of junk that will make your life miserable. Stay safe and take your time making large purchases and big life decisions. If someone tries to hurry you along to make the decision, drop the whole thing, and walk away. Only those with bad intentions will try to rush you about things.

What if a uniformed police officer came up to you and asked you to do something odd or even against the law? Would you do it based solely on his uniform?

You've got to remember that getting a uniform isn't all that hard to do anymore. If someone in a uniform tells you to do something you think isn't right, then you've got every right to not only question them, you've got the right to tell them no.

If you hear something repeatedly from more than one source, are you apt to believe it without looking further into it? This is happening more and more with social media. And more often it's found out to be false rumors rather than the truth.

Do you have trouble saying no – especially when in public?

If you can't say no to things when others are around, then you might fall victim to a scammer. Practice saying no. It might sound silly or even rude to you, but you have opportunities most times to answer a question with no. Maybe the next time you're in the supermarket, and the sample person asks you if you'd like to try something that's on sale, you can just say no, thank you.

Now you've got a list of things to check to see if you do. Be honest with yourself about the things you're doing. If you can't be honest with yourself about things, then you can't be true to yourself when it matters the most – when someone is trying to take advantage of you.

Maybe you aren't one of the people who can get taken advantage of easily. There are signs that you're not easily manipulated too. Test yourself and see how many of these characteristics you have.

Not that you're a jerk, but you expect to be respected. You give respect; you should be the recipient of it as well. If you feel disrespected, you don't take it lightly, and you don't keep quiet about it either. You let the person doing the disrespect know that it will not be tolerated. You call them out on it. If you do this, then pulling the wool over your eyes won't be an easy task.

Do you know what you need and aren't afraid to ask for it? If so, then you've got something some people don't. You aren't a narcissist but know what your needs are and expect them to be met.

If you have an opinion, are you able to express it freely? Not everyone can do this. Being able to speak out loud about things you believe in means you have faith in yourself and your ability to make good decisions. You know you're smart, and you've got self-worth and aren't afraid of ridicule if someone disagrees with your opinion. If a would-be manipulator tries to tell you that you're wrong about something that you know you are right about, you won't back down. You won't get played.

Does it bother you to say no? If you don't have a problem saying no, then you'd be hard to coerce into doing something or believing something a manipulator might try on you.

We all have the right to say no to anything we want and not to give a reason for it. Some of us use this right efficiently, while others of us have a hard time saying no if we can't provide a good and legitimate reason for saying it. Users, manipulators, and scammers will use this against those of us who have a hard time saying no.

You are your first priority. You refuse to let other people's dramatic lives get in the way of your life, and what matters to you. You respect yourself too much to let yourself be drawn into other people's problems – most of which they've brought on themselves. If this describes you, then you really don't have to worry about getting drawn into any dark manipulator's web.

If you have lines that cannot be crossed and someone attempts to do just that, you will deal with them, and there will be consequences they will face. If a coworker attempted to go over your head with something, trying to make you look inadequate at your job so he'd look better at his, you wouldn't take it lightly. You'd let them know that you knew what they were up to and you won't stand for it. "Tell the truth, or you will be dealt with."

The manipulator – much like a bully – will see that you're not to be messed with and will even gain respect for you. You also don't shy away from dealing with a bully. You shut that down right away, letting them know you are not the one to be messed with.

In some cases, a person will try to blame you for something you didn't do. They might say that your actions caused them to fail at something. You know it wasn't you and refused to take the blame.

While you might not have every single one of these strong characteristics, if you have even a quarter of them, you're less likely to become the victim of someone using dark manipulations to get you under their control or to hurt you. You're also less likely to allow anyone you love or care about to be hurt by a manipulator.

It's people who exhibit these qualities and characteristics which those of us with the characteristics of victims can look up to and learn from. All of the things these types of people do are perfectly acceptable and even mentally healthy. We all should strive to gain as many of these traits as we possibly can. It can only benefit us.

You can learn new behaviors. Just because you might not have always been the person to say no, doesn't mean you can't become that person. Just because you've been believing everything on the news doesn't mean it always has to be that way. You can learn new ways. You can learn new ways to deal with things and people. It's never too late to change. Change is good for us – especially when it means we get stronger from it and become less likely to be victims.

What about manipulators? Are you one of those?

The first thing you must ask yourself is this. Have I mastered the art of deception? Am I a great liar? Does lying come second nature to me?

All manipulators must be good liars. It's one of their skills – may be the most important one.

Do you feel you need to control people in order to get what you want? Maybe you feel that you can't accomplish much on your own and you need people to do as you say without asking why. That means bending them a bit, breaking their stubborn streak so they'll just do what you say so that things can get done faster. Lies help ease that process a bit.

You take the truth and turn it around and around until the person you need help from is left confused. You're all too eager to help them understand – help them to see things your way and how it is they can help you. It's all for the greater good, in your mind. If they end up thinking they're crazy, then all the better for you. Now you've got them dependent on you to tell them what's right and what's wrong.

Do you believe that harsh criticism is necessary? Maybe in your eyes, people need to see their faults clearly. If this means they don't have as much self-esteem as they did before, that's even better. You can lead their decisions; they needed help anyway.

Is it necessary to you to be the person that people count on? Is it important to you to put the roof over your family's heads? Those are quality characteristics, right?

In most cases, they are. But if you want to do all that so that you can tell everyone what to do, then it's not mentally healthy for any of you.

It's not easy to look in the mirror and see bad things in your eyes. But it is necessary, to be honest with yourself about your shortcomings. We all have them. There's not one of us who doesn't have at least one of these dark traits.

They bear pointing out, so you know what to look for and work on.

In most situations, are you thinking about how you're affected over how everyone else is being affected? Is it an office party and food brought in for everyone to enjoy? You are lactose intolerant, and all you see are cheeses and ice creams. You're on a strict no-sugar diet, and there are cake and sodas. What are *you* supposed to eat? What are *you* supposed to drink?

In your mind, this seems reasonable. No one thought about you after all. But how you act is critical here. Do you blow up? Do you sull up? Or do you shrug it off? So what if there's nothing there you can eat or drink? Not everyone is on a diet or lactose intolerant. You should be prepared for this since you've got such restrictions on your diet.

You pull out a bottle of water and a veggie tray you keep in the mini fridge in your office for just such an occasion, and you join in the comradery of your coworkers. That is – if you're not a manipulator who tries to throw your weight and temper around to be the center of attention.

What about boundaries? Do you even see them? Do you care about them?

Manipulative people don't pay attention to people's boundaries or space. When in line, do you crowd others? When dealing with someone, do you respect their ideas and beliefs? Or do you force your opinions and beliefs on them?

It's essential to give people their physical and mental space. They have a right to their place in line without you breathing down their neck. And they have a right to their opinions whether you share them or not.

There are times when it is someone else's fault. A person runs a red light and runs into your car. Yes, they are at fault. But what about *you*? Do you take responsibility for *your* mistakes?

When you can't accept the fact that you're human and you too do things wrong and have accidents or make poor decisions, then you've got issues that need to be dealt with. It can't possibly be your fault.

Owning your mistakes, bad decisions, and accidents are important. Blaming others might seem to be taking the light off you, but you're only fooling yourself if you think that.

Do you play on people's emotions? Do you try to make them feel sorry for you so that you can get something out of them or get them to do something for you? This is a basic manipulation. If you think it's right, think about what you'd do if the shoe were on the other foot.

How do you talk about other people? Is it nice? Is it mean? Is it dishonest?

Is it necessary for you that others see you as the best one? Are you willing and able to put people down behind their back, but not tell them the same things to their face?

If this is a thing you do, then you should ask yourself why you're doing it. First of all, it can come back to bite you in the butt. When word gets around that you were talking some ugly stuff about someone, chances are there's a confrontation coming your way. And chances are that you like to avoid things like that.

Being a manipulator can make life a lot harder than it has to be. Not everyone is a pushover. Not everyone will sit down and shut up when you're doling out your own brand of justice or the truth. And not everyone will let you walk away when they come to tell you they won't stand for what you're doing.

Again, we all do at least one of these things, maybe more. All of us should look at manipulating traits we have and try to stop doing them. It's better for all of us if we do.

Chapter 3 : Expressions that Carry Weight

Mental health wasn't always as easy to get information on as it has been since the internet came to life. Psychology, psychiatry, and sociology were things only those who went to college to obtain doctorates understood. The rest of us had to seek professional help if we felt we or someone we loved had mental problems. That's no longer the case. This has both good and bad aspects to it.

Once upon a time, when Junior began to exhibit irrational behavior, his parents took him to see a physician who would refer him to a specialist, perhaps a psychiatrist. This professional would help Junior to get better through therapy and maybe even pharmaceuticals.

With online information, many people are self-medicating, self-evaluating, and self-sabotaging. Most people don't look at themselves the way others see them. We tend to hide our darkest parts from ourselves – turn a blind eye to what we blatantly do wrong. That makes taking on our mental problems alone an exceptionally bad idea. We need the professionals to evaluate us, give us therapeutic help, and yes, even drugs if need be.

We throw around expressions about mental health as if we're highly educated about these things. 'She's bipolar. He's a narcissist. You're a psycho.' It's easy to say these things now that we all believe we have at least a healthy amount of knowledge about these mental conditions. But are we playing with what amounts to loaded guns?

The words we spout with such ease, carry a lot of weight. Being called a narcissist can be quite hurtful. Before you go dishing out these words, you should take a hard look at them – really educate yourself on what these terms mean. We're all a bit fragile, ego-wise. Most people have self-doubts, even if they don't talk about them.

Telling someone, they're mentally deranged might push someone with an actual mental disorder over the edge. You wouldn't want to be standing there with fresh words on your lips that prove to flip the switch on someone with psychosis.

Understanding the truth behind these powerful words should help you gain proper respect for them. You don't want to end up being that poor guy in the morgue who had to let his crazy girlfriend know just how crazy he thought she really was.

Manipulation is the cornerstone for the dark triad; narcissism, psychopathy, and Machiavellianism. Understanding manipulation and how it's done by a person with a mental disorder is critical.

Manipulation is a thing that's around us most of the time. Advertisements are meant to catch your attention; make you believe what's said about a product and purchase it. This isn't anything evil. It's just the way people have figured out to sell things.

It's the underhanded manipulations that are hidden in the words and actions of a person with a mental disorder that can hurt you, even make you feel that you're the crazy one.

It may take you some time to realize what's been happening to you. It might even take you by surprise. What reaction you will have in finding out someone's been covertly manipulating you is what will either save or destroy you.

Every action has a reaction; this, we all know. Smart people try to see the ripples of responses before they make the first wave. Self-preservation is vital when taking steps against a person with a real mental disorder. And if they've been professionally diagnosed, then all the more reason to tread with caution.

In the fictitious manipulation case of Dan and Mable Smith, Mable is the one with the disorder and Dan – her husband of twenty years – is the man with a problem on his hands.

Dan's mother was a strong woman who raised him and his four brothers all on her own after their father died at the young age of thirty-five. Used to women with more spunk than most, Dan met and fell in love with a savvy young woman while in college.

Mable got a degree in kinesiology; she wanted to be a physical education teacher. Dan earned a degree in history and wanted to become a teacher after graduation. The two had similar interests and married not long after graduation. They found a high school in a nearby town where they could both work. Mable was determined to find a place they could both teach at – she couldn't bear the thought of not seeing her husband off and on throughout the day.

"Hey, hubby," Mable greeted Dan as she entered his empty classroom. "Got a sec for me?"

Although papers stacked high on his desk, Dan pushed them aside to pay attention to his wife of five years now. "Of course, I do."

Mable pushed his chair back, took a seat on his lap, then kissed his lips softly. "I've missed you."

Laughing, Dan had become used to this term. "It's been all of two hours since you saw me last."

"Well, I love you so much is why." Mable's lips brushed his cheek. "How about steaks for dinner tonight?"

"That sounds great to me."

Hopping off his lap, Mable sauntered away from him, heading to the door. "Great. Stop at Mike's Butcher Shop and pick some up. Then you can grill them up around six tonight. I'd love a salad and baked potato with mine. Make sure you fully cook the steaks, Dan. I don't want to see a hint of pink." She turned to wink at him. "And not on yours either. Promise me."

Dan loved rare steaks but knew better than to open that can of worms with his wife. "I know, honey. But, I kind of thought you meant that *you'd* be making the steaks. You were the one who brought it up after all."

"Me?" her laughter peeled through the air as she shook her head. "Don't be silly, Dan. You know you make them much better than I do."

"Well, maybe you could make the potatoes and the salads then?" His day would be long and tiresome with all the tests he had to grade. Making dinner – especially one out on the grill – wasn't a thing he'd had in mind.

"Can't," Mable said as she slipped out the door. "I'll be home about six-thirty. Have dinner ready by then. Love you." And then she was gone.

Five years later and Dan is sitting on the back porch, rocking in his oversized chair while watching the sunrise. It's a gorgeous morning, and all he can think about is going fishing.

Mable's voice comes from inside the house, "Dan? Dan, where are you?"

"Out here, honey." He smiles as he thinks about taking his little kayak out on the smooth as glass lake behind their home.

The backdoor squeaks open, and Mable's face peers out at him. "I want to clean the house today."

"Okay." He sips the warm coffee he made after getting up an hour earlier than his wife. Sometimes he just needs space and time away from her.

"Can you get the ladder out?" she asks as she looks briefly at the pink sky. "I want you to wash the windows."

"I thought you said that *you* wanted to clean the house today?" Dan's plans didn't entail such activity on this beautiful day. "I wanted to take the boat out and get in some fishing. It's going to be one of the prettiest days on record."

"Well, if you get the house cleaned in time, then I guess you can do that." Mable opens the door wide to show Dan that she's dressed and ready to leave. "I'm going to go do some shopping. I have no idea when I'll get back home. When I do get back, I want to see everything sparkling clean. The fridge needs cleaning out. The laundry has stacked up. And the yard needs mowing too. But you can get to that tomorrow. Today is all about the inside of the house."

"But," Dan tries to say.

One finger held up tells him that Mable isn't going to listen. "Honey, I *need* your help with this. I've got to do the shopping for our annual Fourth of July party. Your mom and brothers are coming next week, and I just want everything to be perfect."

"You know what?" Dan comes up with. "I'll tell them we're not going to do the party this year. We can all just meet up somewhere to watch a spectacular firework show. That way you and I won't have to do so much work. The lake really is calling my name, baby."

The hand moving to her hip, lets Dan know his wife is not on board with his great idea. "Not today. And we *are* going to have a party. Stop being lazy and selfish, Dan. Now get up and get started on the housework. There's a lot of it to do, and it's not getting done with you sitting on your butt out here on the porch."

Ten years later – their twentieth wedding anniversary:

Dan's back is injured, and he's been stuck in bed for a week. Mable's tired of doing everything for him, and she's just about had enough. "Look, I think you need to move around; get some exercise."

"The doctor said that I needed to rest my back for two weeks. It's only been one week. I'm not about to hurt it again." Dan fell off a ladder while cleaning the gutters of the house, the injury to his back was so substantial he had to spend a couple of days in the hospital where they thought they might have to do surgery. "I don't want to go under the knife. I'm going to follow the doctor's sage advice, Mable."

"I am a kinesiology degree holder, Dan. I think I know what I'm talking about. Exercise is what you need. And I can't run this house all on my own." Mable exhales loudly. "You're making more out of this back thing than you need to. It's awfully selfish of you to leave me doing everything."

Anger seeps into Dan's brain. He's dealt with his wife for twenty years, done almost every chore imaginable, and *she's* calling *him* selfish? He's had it. "Look, if I'm a burden to you, then maybe you should just leave me." Sometimes he wishes that she would just leave him. Life would be so much easier that way.

Narrowing her eyes, Mable can see she's lost the upper hand somehow. "*I'm* not going anywhere. Now, you listen to me, Dan. You *will* get out of that bed, and you *will* do the exercises that I tell you will help your back. Neither of us is leaving – so get that out of your mind right now. Until death do us part, remember?"

Death would be a pleasant relief in Dan's opinion. "Mable, you're a controlling narcissist. I'm done with being your puppet. I'm not getting out of the bed my doctor told me to stay in for two weeks. Just leave me alone."

"What did you call me?" Mable can't believe the words he's said.

"A controlling narcissist! Now, leave me alone."

One year later...

"It's a real shame for Dan. How are you holding up, Mable?" Joe, a fellow coach from the school she works at, asks her.

"I'm doing okay. It's hard without him. He was such a great husband. He did it all, took care of me so well that I'm spoiled now." Her eyes scan the cemetery. "If he would've just followed his doctor's advice and stayed in bed, then he'd still be here with me today. The poor man had to try to get up, try to help me out with the housework. His heart just gave out on him."

"You know, I can help you out, Mable. It's been a year. Maybe it's time you let Dan go. I'm right here, you know."

Smiling, Mable can see it in Joe's eyes – he adores her and will do anything she tells him to. "Maybe you're right, Joe. How about you come over tonight? You can bring steaks and cook them on the grill."

Persuasion is another term that carries a lot of weight. Some people use persuasion in only the best of ways, while others use it to get others to do things they normally wouldn't. In these cases, persuasive actions must be seen early on, or you might become a victim.

Lying in bed after a torrid sexual session, Lydia knows the time is right to ask Manuel to do what she's wanted him to for some time now. "So, you know how my father's been keeping the car from me, right?"

"Yeah." Manuel kisses her on top of the head as he holds her in his arms.

"So, I thought that maybe you could get into the garage somehow and get it out for me." She chews on her lower lip, trying to look nervous.

"Breaking and entering, plus grand theft auto?" He chuckles. "Who do you think I am?"

"Yeah, it's too much to ask." She sighs, sadly.

"Yeah, it is." Manuel knows Lydia hasn't even spoken to her parents in almost a year. He couldn't possibly break in and steal something she says is hers.

"It's just that I *need* that car. And it's *mine*. My father shouldn't have taken it away. I deserve that car. I worked for that car. It's mine!"

"Is it in your name?" he asks as she sounds so desperate.

"No. Dad wouldn't put it in my name. He's always used it to control me. Well, try to anyway. I won't allow him to do that to me. Not anymore. His reign of terror over me is over. But I need that car." Lydia can sense Manuel's empathy beginning to set in.

"You've said your dad was controlling before. But did he ever hurt you? You know, physically?"

"Yes." She senses that if Manuel believes her father did her very wrong, that he might get her the car the way she wants him to. "His beatings were things I'd rather forget; unfortunately, nightmares of them persist at times."

"Beatings?" Manuel hugs her, feeling terrible for her.

"Yes. I'm just glad I've gotten away from him and that awful home. And if I had my car, I could get a job and not be so dependent on you to get me to work and stuff."

"Yeah, but I could end up in jail if I do what you want me to, Lydia." Manuel kisses the side of her head. "If you keep working, then you'll have money to buy yourself a car soon. Don't even think about that car your father gave you."

"You make it sound easy, but it's not. I've got other bills to pay, Manuel. If I can find out when my parents are going out of town, then you could get the car without anyone knowing." Lydia feels like she's got Manuel close to doing what she wants. "It's a whole other state, Manuel. How could you get caught? I would do it myself, but I'm not strong enough to pry that garage door open. And my parents don't know you. If they've put in a surveillance system, they won't be able to say who stole the car. Come on, honey. Please."

A month later...

Hard knocks at the door startle Manuel who's home alone. "Who the hell is it?"

"The police," comes a firm voice on the other side of the door. "Open up, or we'll break this door down. You're under arrest, and I think you know why, Manuel."

Emotional influence sounds menacing - only because it is. Using your fake emotions to spark someone else's is pretty insidious. Take the fictional case of Abby, who has run over the neighbor's dog while texting on her phone.

The solid thump under her car jolts Abby back into reality. "What the hell was that?" Putting her cell phone down, she slows down and looks in her review mirror to find a dark heap lying on the pavement. "Oh, no!"

Pulling to the side of the street, Abby gets out and runs to find her neighbor, Twila's, dog. He's not breathing; his brown eyes stare at nothing, his long red tongue hangs from his mouth. "No!"

She didn't mean to hit the dog. But Twila will be so angry with her if she knows she was on the phone when she hit him. She's got to do something – anything – to get Twila's sympathy, rather than her anger.

Gathering her thoughts, Abby begins to run to Twila's house. Crying hysterically, she bangs on her neighbor's door.

Twila opens the door, wondering what the onslaught of tears is about. "Abby? What's wrong?"

"He was crazy, Twila. I don't know why he did it!" Abby falls to her knees.

"Who?" Twila stoops to help her back up. "What's happened, Abby?"

"He came out of nowhere. He darted in front of me. I stepped on the brakes, tried not to," a sob interrupts her words as she buries her face in Twila's chest.

Hugging her neighbor, Twila feels worried and sympathetic. "Twila, just tell me what's happened and to whom. Please."

Turning slowly, Abby points to the dark lump on the street. "Over there. He's over there, Twila. I'm so sorry. I tried my best to avoid him, but he ran straight into my car."

Twila's eyes take in the sad sight. "Spot ran into your car?"

"Yes. I'm so sorry," Abby cries.

"It's not your fault, Abby. Come on. It's going to be okay," Twila consoles her neighbor. "I know you didn't do it on purpose."

No, Abby didn't hit the dog on purpose, but she did hit it out of neglect to watch where she was going. Not that Twila will ever find that out.

The darkest form of mental manipulation has to be mind control and NLP – Neuro-Linguistic Programming. Both of these things can be used for good purposes, think helping you to quit smoking or stick to a diet to make yourself healthier. But they can also be used to gain control of others, even large numbers of people.

Cult leaders use this type of manipulation to get their followers to do as they want. Phrases are repeated over and over again to get them stuck in the minds of their followers.

Religious figures have also been known to use these things to drill into the minds of their congregations the ideals they want them to have. And using something as powerful as the Bible or some other form of religious literature only serves to make their words hold more weight.

Still, politicians use these things to get people to vote for them or the things they want. Saying the same things over and over, giving stories, some of which might be false, to gain sympathy or compassion is also a technique used in this practice.

If you find yourself at a political rally, and the main speaker keeps chanting a specific phrase, you might think about pulling yourself back out of that for a moment to monitor the behavior of the crowd. Ask yourself some questions as you watch, while not becoming emotionally involved. Is the energy or vibe a bit overzealous? Is the overall feeling one of negativity? Is the phrase meant to draw out anger in people? What is the message the speaker is trying to convey? Is it good or bad? Could this message incite a riot?

While it's perfectly okay to put yourself behind a person who has a mission that you agree with, it's essential to make sure *you* have decided to go along with it. Be sure that you have used your own judgment and did the research to make an educated decision about following this leader on his quest.

There *are* things worth fighting for, there are causes that deserve your help, and there are some that aren't worth it or aren't things you would agree on without being mentally manipulated. It's easier to do than you might think.

The onslaught of fake news is one-way influential figures are using mind control and NLP to force their control over others, using scare tactics to feed the brains of those who refuse to do the fact-checking that must be done before one goes off on a tangent about anything.

Take this real example. In 1938, a young actor/producer bent on making a name for himself did a fake news broadcast of H.G. Wells' sci-fi novel, War of the Worlds. Orson Welles did a remarkable job of making the whole thing sound like he was doing a live broadcast as Mars attacked Earth.

As this was all done on the radio, some people believed the broadcast to be real, and panic ensued. Some reports, after the show ended, were of suicides, people leaving their homes in fear, and mass hysteria. Orson Wells had to make an apology the next day about the show that was never meant to be thought of as real. There were things said before and after the show that told the listening audience that this was only a dramatic reading and not real in the least.

What's worse, is that years later, researchers found that there weren't that many reports from people who actually believed that show. Even the reports on the mass hysteria caused by the fake news show weren't accurate. But for many years people believed all of it. They believed that people killed themselves after hearing that Mars was invading Earth. They believed those entire families fled their homes with wet cloths covering their mouths to stay safe from the poison gas the Martians used to kill the Earthlings. People believed it all, and that shows you just how easy it is for someone to get into people's heads and make them think things that couldn't possibly be true.

Chapter 4 : What Makes People Tick

The first step to understanding anything about dark behavior is knowing what makes people tick. One must know the truths behind human thinking – even if that means we have to see things about ourselves that we might not like.

The majority of people are only thinking about themselves most of the time. What can you do for me? How will what I do for you, help me? What's in it for me?

I'm sure you've asked yourself these questions and even more self-serving queries in the past. This, by no means, means that you have any of the dark triad's mental disorders, this only means that you are human. As humans, we have the natural instinct to protect ourselves and get what we need to survive. Survival instincts are things we're born with. We just have different ideas about what it takes to survive is all.

Most of us also have compassion, empathy, and charity that go along with the selfish parts of us, but we all have selfish elements. Looking inward will allow you to see more in others. If you can see something in yourself, then you can certainly spot it in others.

This doesn't mean that whatever your particular darkness is that there's the same darkness in everyone else. We all have our own demons, our own darkness to deal with.

Some people lie about everything. Some of these people think it's perfectly natural to lie and that everyone does it all the time. While we all have to lie from time to time, that doesn't make us all liars who lie about everything.

The same can be said for those people who cheat on their significant others. A lot of people who find it okay to cheat, think everyone else does it as well, they just haven't gotten caught yet.

It's these types of behaviors and trains of thought that one must look out for. If you meet a person who truly believes that everyone lies about everything all the time, then you can bet they don't believe you, and they will not be honest with you. This will let you know not to waste your time and energy on that person, right from the start. You can move on without second-guessing yourself for doing so.

Since not all people are honest and open, you must learn to listen to what's *not* being said. Read body language and take everything said with a grain of salt until you truly know a person. Don't judge a book by its cover, whether that cover is very nice or extremely tattered. What's on the outside doesn't always reflect what's on the inside. Some of the nicest looking people can have the darkest hearts while some of the least attractive people can house qualities of the purest nature.

While we now know that most people are only looking out for themselves, how can we get past that aspect of a person?

Along with this selfish aspect of ourselves comes the need to be seen as a good person. One might assume it to be a difficult task to be selfish and good at the same time. But it's not hard when you think about why we do nice things in the first place.

While it's best to do nice things and to never expect any repayment of any kind for that act, people seldom practice this. There's usually something there in the back of a person's mind that has a reason for doing something nice - even if that reason is only to make them feel proud of themselves for doing something so selfless.

Maybe you're taking the other side, for instance, thinking that you are not selfish. You may think about your kids all the time and do for them -

before you will do for yourself. And while that's admirable, it's not selfless.

That child is a part of you, a part that you want to make sure succeeds in life. So, of course, you'll let them eat the last spoonful of green beans even if you're still hungry. Your child has growing to do, and you want that child to grow up strong and healthy.

Why is that, if we all mostly care about ourselves?

Our genes reside in those children, and we want our genes to go on and on and on. That's why we raise our children to do better than we did. We will be their safety net, their springboard, their biggest fans, whatever it takes to make sure our genes go on and on, we will do it.

Maybe you have no children and never care to. Perhaps you have no want to see your genes go on and on. Once again, you are thinking about yourself more than you're thinking about anyone else. You don't care that humanity needs to proliferate, the same as any other creature on this planet does. That task, or burden, can be someone else's to bear.

None of these things makes you a bad person; you're just a human being is all. And these little dark things inside all of us are things that people with lots of darkness inside use to point out how they're not as bad as others claim them to be. We're all bad in one way or another; why should they feel bad about how they are?

The thing about people with dark traits, such as the dark triad, is that they lack some of the key things the rest of us have; empathy, remorse, and a sense of right and wrong.

Okay, so now you know that all humans are self-absorbed to some degree. What else do you need to know about people that will tell you what makes a particular person tick?

Perhaps you meet a person who has dominating qualities. Why do they have them? What makes them think that being dominate will get them what they want in life? And what is it that they really want anyway?

People who dominate have a goal in mind. They want to show others how in control and prepared they are. They have it all together and have acquired things others need. They use these attributes to give to others, then expect their recipients to do things for them as well. And not all dominating people have evil intent. Some merely have goals in mind that make sense to them. In their opinions, there is only room for one person at the top. From the top, they are more than happy to let what they've accumulated trickle down – all at a pace they decide best for all. And this way of life works for some people on both ends of this spectrum.

Some people don't know how to get what they need in life. They need to depend on someone else. Who better than a dominate person to help ease the stresses life has to offer?

Another train of thought is old; I'll scratch your back if you scratch mine. Now, this works for a lot of people. They are open and honest about what they will do for you and what they expect you to do for them. If you both agree, then you've struck a deal to make life easier on you both.

In this way of life, there's no one leader, you both lead, you both have responsibilities you take on, and you both expect the other to stand up to what they said they'll do.

In other cases, trading works out for people. I have something you want; you have something I want, so let's trade. It's not ideal for everyone, but for some people, it works.

The thing about all of these ways of thinking and living life is that each tactic is used by people with the mental disorders of the dark triad. But they take these traits to new heights and then there's also the lack of good characteristics that level out the bad ones.

To find out what makes a person tick, establish the way they think in one of the ways above. Once you know that about a person, you can understand where they're coming from and where they intend to go.

Before you ever think about finding out what makes someone else tick, you've got to know what makes you tick. Why try to understand anyone else when you can't even understand yourself?

This requires you to do a bit of soul-searching. Are you a person who steps up to the plate more often than others? Are you the guy who lingers in the background, waiting and hoping someone else will want to step up to the plate? Or are you the person who's on their cell, not even aware there's a plate that needs stepping up to?

In this scenario, you've got a dominant personality, the one who willingly steps up. You've got the submissive person, the one hoping someone else will step up. And you've got that person who's going to sit back and see what happens. If you must step up, you'll be sure to make some assurances that someone will be helping you out in some way. You're the trader or the, you scratch my back, and I'll scratch your kind of person.

If you're a natural dominant, you won't want to pick a trader as a partner in anything. These two people won't see eye on eye on much. A dominate needs submissive people, that's just the way it goes. And a trader needs another trader or back scratcher – a submissive won't do for them either. They want someone to share the load with – they don't wish to carry it all, while some passive person sits and looks timid about the task at hand.

And you must remember that it takes all kinds of people - with their little quirks - to make the world go around. How boring it would be if everyone were the same. And not much would get accomplished if the world was full of dominators – or submissives. Even a world full of traders wouldn't work out. We need our leaders, and those often come in the form of a dominating personality trait.

Relationships are another thing people think about a lot. Even if a person likes a mostly solitary lifestyle, they still think about relationships. Sure, it may be the relationship they have with the television, but they think about it. I wonder if the TV is missing me while I'm busy taking a bath. I should really get back to that as soon as I can.

People wonder what other people in their lives are thinking about. But not all the things they could be thinking about. People wonder if those they are involved with or have been involved with in the past, think about them often or at all.

I'm sure you've had someone in your past who's no longer a part of your life. I'm positive you've thought about them at times and wondered if they ever thought about you. They most likely have, and most likely in the same way you did. They wondered if you'd ever thought about them and the times you two shared.

When people connect, be it friendships, romantic relationships, or even work relationships, they form a bond of sorts. You will always be thought about from time to time – and if you have current relationships, you will be thought about more often. By the same token, you will think more often about people you're dealing with at the present than you will about people from your past. It's just human nature to do so.

Learning how to spot the tell-tell signs of someone's innate character will help you to determine which people you will give a shot to and which you won't. Once again, you must be truthful about the type of person you are first, to know whom you will and won't get along with well.

A dominant person is pretty easy to spot. They will stand up straight and tall. They will seek eye contact, as they will also be sizing up any new people they meet as well. A firm handshake, a friendly smile that's not too broad and welcoming, and straightforward ways of communication will help you see the dominate inside the new person you're meeting.

Submissive people tend to be rather shy and unobtrusive. They often have to be spoken to first, rather than them starting a conversation. Their handshake will be soft, and maybe they won't even want to shake hands at all. Eye contact doesn't come easy for them, so they will avert their eyes often, only taking short glances into another person's eyes.

The traders or back scratchers of this world have tendencies of both dominates and submissives. They can look you straight in the eyes, then suddenly feel it's a bit too much and look away. They also will have moderately firm handshakes. They're easier to talk to as well as they tend to listen much more than the other types of people.

Not any one of these types are better than the other, so it doesn't matter which one you are. All of us have plenty of other aspects to our personalities to make us distinct. But understanding the core trait of someone's – and your own - personality is a great thing. It can make life easier for you, in the long run.

Just think how many failed relationships you might've never even tried if you'd looked into your own core personality trait and that of the person you tried to make something with. Now, some of those relationships might've taught you invaluable lessons. I'll bet that one of them was that you would never get involved with anyone who had their core traits again.

See – you've just gained some time-saving knowledge right here.

Chapter 5 : Techniques of Dark Psychology You Might Not Be Aware Of

Those people who have traits of the disorders in the Dark Triad also can hide the darkest parts of themselves for a while. They must lure people in after all. One can't possibly lure in a victim if they are acting like a deranged lunatic.

If you find yourself with a person who starts to exhibit some of the things you're about to learn, you might want to take a step back and reevaluate your relationship before it gets any deeper. Not that most of these people will let you move on without a fight, but at least you can know what to look for.

Love flooding is a term that sounds nice. In the right doses, it can be. But a person with dark intentions doesn't do it in small doses, and they don't do it because they love you. You've got to remember that people with these disorders are incapable of love in a way that's healthy. They seek to take you over completely, drain you, use you, abuse and manipulate you, your thoughts, your entire life.

Being held, kissed, hugged, told how special you are to a person just feels good. And after an argument, it's pretty standard for romantic couples to make up, starting with something like this.

But what if this happens a lot, like every day, and for no apparent reason?

What if your significant other adds a little thing like, 'No one will ever love you as much as I do,' what would you think about that?

What if you're told, 'No matter what, I'll never let you go? Not ever. So, don't even try to run away from me and the love I have for you,' how would that make you feel?

You've probably heard things like that in horror movies. One minute, the guy is holding his girl, cuddling, kissing, hugging, and whispering sweet words to her. Then he's saying something pretty ominous, all while still holding her tight in his strong arms.

In essence, he's flooding her with love, so much love that she can't ever walk away from it. One would undoubtedly feel overwhelmed, and one would be right to.

Before someone pulls this on their victim, they will have to be sure they've got a strong enough hold on them. Love denial isn't a thing one should play around with when the relationship is too new. It would be very easy to let them keep on denying you if that was the case.

Say you've had a tiny spat, nothing to merit the cold shoulder treatment. Take this fictitious scene:

"Lila, can you put my things in the laundry this morning before you go to work, honey?" John asks, sweetly.

But Lila is running late, a half-hour late, due to John's insistence that they make love that morning – even though they both woke up later than normal. "Oh, honey, I can't. I've gotta run. Sorry."

Without saying a word, John leaves the room. And Lila doesn't think anything about it, at the time. But later, when she calls him at lunch to see how his day is going, he sends her call straight to voicemail. She shoots him a sweet text – Loved this morning with you, call me later when you get a chance. –

By the end of the workday, she's still had no reply to the text. She tries calling again on her way home – still sent to voicemail right away. And when she comes home, he's not there. And he won't be there until much later than usual.

"John! There you are," Lila exclaims when he finally comes home.

John's eyes are void of emotion, his body language is staunch, and his lips form a thin line. Walking right past her, he doesn't say a thing, merely makes a slight humph sound.

"John?" Lila asks as she has no clue what's wrong with him. "Is there something wrong?"

When he walks away from her, leaving her alone, she knows something has to be wrong. But what?

Later, she goes to bed, and he's already in bed, sleeping. The next morning he's gone before she gets up. Lila doesn't even try to text or call; she has no idea what to say or ask. She's upset, feeling insecure about their future and unsure of why he's shutting her out this way.

Another day and night go by before he utters a thing to her. Lila's done his laundry as a way of making some kind of amends for whatever she's done to make him so angry with her. "I've got your laundry done. I'll just put it away for you."

"See?" he finally asks. "Was that so hard to do?"

Stunned, Lila stares at him blankly. "Is that why you haven't spoken to me in days? Because I didn't have time to start your laundry the other morning?"

"I think you know the answer to that." Pulling her in for a hug, he kisses the tip of her nose. "I should always be more important to you than anything or anyone else, Lila. It makes me unhappy when you don't put me first."

You can see how if Lila wasn't too involved in their relationship, she would've never stuck around to see why John was acting the way he was. But he'd lured her in, made her feel loved, wanted, needed. Once he's sure of her devotion, he is able to be who he really is. It won't be the last time she's the recipient of love denial if she stays with him.

Coercive reinforcement is a common way to parent – although many psychologists don't agree with this method of training a child to do what you want them to. Positive reinforcement is the approved method for that.

When someone in a romantic relationship plays this card, it's nothing short of mental abuse. Case in point:

Clair has a job that pays well and her boyfriend, Greg, works at an entry-level position, making minimum wage. She's got a surprise for her man. "Greg, come out here. I've got something for you."

Greg comes outside after hearing his girl call out for him. "You've got something for me?" As he opens the door, his eyes land on a brand-new truck. "No way!"

Nodding and laughing, Clair shouts, "Yes! It's all yours, Greg. I knew you needed a car and got you one."

Although Greg is ecstatic about having a new truck, he's a little worried about the hold Clair will have on him. "You're not going to try to take it away if I don't do something you want, are you? Like you did with the dog you gave me last year. You gave him away when I refused to go with you to your parents' house for Easter."

Crossing her arms over her chest, she smiles at him wickedly. "Now, Greg, why would I do that? Here, take the keys; she's all yours."

And things go okay for a while. But then Greg goes out after work with the guys one evening and comes home a bit late with beer on his breath. "Sorry, I'm late, Clair. I brought pizza, so you don't have to worry about dinner."

Holding her hand out, she wiggles her fingers. "The keys, Greg."

Greg's confused. "Why?"

"You went out. You didn't ask me if you could go out." She wiggles her fingers again. "The keys."

"I've gone out plenty of times after work to have a couple of beers with the guys." Greg's not happy about what his girlfriend is trying to do here.

"Not in *my* car; you haven't." Claire's not going to give in. "The keys. Now."

Pulling them out of his pocket, he asks, "When will I get them back?"

"Whenever I think you've learned how to ask before you go out, instead of just letting me know after the fact." She takes the keys and puts them away and won't be giving them back for a week for what he's done.

Arguing is healthy and even something that couples must do in order to learn how to live together. But when one person takes that arguing to a whole new level, then something just might be a lot more wrong than the other knew.

Take this fictitious example:

"Bob, for the love of God, just drop it." Jan is done with this argument that's gone on for over an hour.

"How can I drop it?" Bob's not about to just let this end without her seeing his side and agreeing with it. "You don't like the color of the lawn chairs. I love burnt orange, and I want you to like it too. I have lots of plans for the backyard, and that color is the base for the whole thing."

"I've told you and told you, Bob. The backyard is both of ours. We need to meet in the middle here. My favorite color is blue. You don't see me telling you that we've got to do it in blue. So, stop telling me we've got to do it in that awful orange color. You can take the chairs back and get the tan ones. That's called compromise, Bob."

"I won't do it. I won't let you do it, either. I want a burnt orange, and that's that. I won't give up, Jan. I'll keep this thing going all night if I have to."

Jan's weary of fighting with her husband. She knows well how long he can go on and on without ever tiring out. "Fine. Have it your way. You will, anyway."

"Good."

Tiring someone out just to get your way isn't fighting fair or a nice thing to do to someone you're supposed to love and want to share your life with. Compromise is the cornerstone of a healthy relationship. This means that sometimes each person gets to have things their way, but when it's serious, or expensive, compromise is better than one person getting their way.

We've all been victims of subliminal coercion. Advertisements use this type of thing all the time. We've come to expect it out of things like that. But when a loved one does it, it can be hurtful.

Most people like it when others are straightforward with them. If you're in a relationship with someone, you like to think they feel they can talk to you about anything. If they want something, you'd expect them to ask you upfront and not try to get what they want by mentally manipulating you.

It's especially dark when your other half wants you to do something. They know you are against. They might leave around some pamphlets about the thing you don't want to do. They might point out how someone else is doing it. Little by little, they're luring you in, making you more and more comfortable about talking about this thing you didn't want to talk about before.

Before you know it, you're doing this thing you were so against, and you might be feeling bad about yourself for getting drawn into it. What's worse, you were drawn in by a person who is supposed to love you and value your feelings and your morals.

The act of choice restriction might not sound that bad. If you're an adult and happen to know that there are lots of choices for most things in this world, even the option of merely not picking anything at all, then it can be hurtful when a loved one does it to you.

Parents do this all the time with their kids. That's understandable. If you're making lunch and all you've got is peanut butter and jelly or ham to make sandwiches with, you've got to give the kids the choices. You can't just make them whatever they want after all.

But when you're adults, and you tell your significant other that there are three houses they can pick from, no other home will do, and they must choose one, that's not only uncool, it's mentally abusive.

Reverse psychology doesn't seem that bad of a thing to do to get someone to do things your way. But when you play games with a person's mind, it not only hurts them, it makes them not trust you.

Mind games are one of the biggest turn-offs in the romantic department. Both men and women hate being the victim of a person who adores playing mind games. The ghosting, the arguing over misunderstandings, the refusal to be honest about emotions, and feelings, gets old quick.

When a person doesn't stop playing the field while dating someone seriously, then you've got a problem. Someone who has to keep the door open for other opportunities and other love interests isn't ever going to give you a hundred percent. If someone can't commit a hundred percent, then you shouldn't accept that. You're worth that amount of commitment. Of course, I'm talking about after you've dated for a while and have given each other plenty of time to really get to know the other.

Rushing is also another thing you have to watch out for. Why the big rush?

Most things you're being rushed to do are mainly because the rusher knows he's got damaged goods he's trying to sell you. And this may be the person themselves who are the damaged goods. Don't rush into anything – buying a car, a house, or anything else that's important and something you will be spending time in for years to come. That includes a relationship.

Brainwashing sounds creepy. That's because it is. Being the victim of brainwashing isn't something people generally worry about. Most think they can't be brainwashed, and some of them are right. Not everyone will be susceptible to becoming a victim of this type of mental manipulation and abuse. But it doesn't mean you've got to be dimwitted to become a victim, either.

Most cases of brainwashing involve holding someone captive for a period of time. There may be physical torture, meant to weaken the body, mind, and spirit so that they can put their message into a person's brain easier. This might be the message that those they've followed before weren't good or honest people. They need to follow their captors – people who know what's best for them.

Still, other abusers won't go as far as torturing their victims. They might use other ways to get people under their spell. Cult leaders have done both physical abuse and other manipulations like The use of sex, drugs, and other forms of things. Some people like a lot can be used to drain a person and replace what they've lost with the ideas the abuser wants them to think of as their own.

Cult leaders want their followers to leave their families behind. This means they've got to turn them against their own parents somehow. The victim is repeatedly told how bad of a person they are, but they're not really to blame for their bad behavior. No, that's their parents' faults. They brought them up in an immoral home. It was the parents who tried to ruin them. All the leader wants to do is help them live the life they were meant to. A life where they give to the whole of the commune and don't think so selfishly. They give whatever their leader needs. He – alone – knows what's best for them all.

When you strip someone of their family, when you tell them they're bad and that their parents made them that way, it takes something out of a person. Even though they may not believe the words the brainwasher is telling them at first, through repetition, they begin to believe it. They begin to hate their parents for making them into something so terrible. And they turn to the leader to show them the true way.

If you're in a relationship and your partner is always accusing you of cheating – even though you never have and didn't think you'd ever be the kind of person who'd do that – you might find yourself growing tired of the accusations. You might find yourself saying that if they don't stop, you'll prove them right. You might find yourself flirting back when someone flirts with you – your better half thinks that's what you've been doing anyway. You always have to defend yourself, why not have a real reason to?

That's why it's important to know when and how to stop things when you see them going in a bad direction. If you're accused of cheating and know that you've never done a thing to warrant that, then you need to let your partner know that you will not tolerate that anymore. If they do it again, you will be forced to end the relationship as it's turning toxic.

If your partner gives you the silent treatment, then you need to let them know you will not tolerate it. You will have to stand your ground about the fact that giving the cold shoulder isn't a healthy way to settle your arguments or let someone know you're not pleased with their behavior.

Once you have established that you won't be going down an unhealthy road with the person in your life, you might find them losing interest in you. Let them. You weren't the victim they were looking for anyway. And if they don't have a real disorder, then they will know what your lines are and won't try to cross them if it means losing you.

If you think arguing extensively with someone who tries to manipulate, you will work and, in the end, you will both be happy, you are only fooling yourself. Arguing has it's time and place, of course. But when someone is trying to manipulate you, you've got to remain calm. You have to let them know you will not be manipulated and if that's their thing, then they can be on their way. Fighting over it, angrily, only gives the situation energy. You've got to snuff that flame out quickly, don't add fuel to the fire and things will work out for you – with or without that person.

Chapter 6 : Nasty Tricks

Emotional manipulation isn't always so easy to spot. After all, the person doing the manipulating is messing with your core emotions. Speaking to your heart, yanking your strings, and getting to that part of you that houses the most empathy, sympathy, and overall concerns are how they get into your head.

When someone gets into your head, it's hard to know if *you're* making the decisions or if *they* are. A great emotional manipulator will make you think it's you who's coming up with the ideas, when it's really them who are pulling strings, making you their puppet.

Let's start with a fictional case that you're sure to have experienced at least once in your life. And maybe you've been the one to use this type of manipulation and didn't even really understand what it was that you were doing. That's because some children use this type of thing to get what they want.

Betty is hanging out on the playground with Sally. She and Sally have only recently begun a friendship. Betty's best friend is a girl named Beth, that's whom she's usually hung out with before Sally moved to their town.

When Beth comes out of her classroom to find Sally and Betty playing together once again, the third time in a row, she's instantly angry. "Why is she playing with that girl again? I'm Betty's best friend. She used to wait for me to get out of class before going to the playground. Now she's always already there with that Sally girl. I hate that girl. She's so prissy and not like Betty and me at all. So, why's Betty hanging out with her all of a sudden?"

John, a boy in Beth's class, overhears Beth's little conversation with herself and offers his sage advice, "Beth, you should just be happy that there's another kid who wants to hang out with you both. Don't be jealous."

"Jealous?" Beth is anything by that, or so she thinks. "I'm not jealous. It's just that Sally isn't like Betty and me. We're like tomboys and Sally is so - not."

"Still, she's hanging with you guys, and she's nice," John offers. "Plus, you girls need someone to help you understand what it means to be a girl. You're about to be twelve. It's about time you two started being a little more like girls and not so much like boys."

A swift punch to John's arm lets him know Beth doesn't agree with him. "You shut up, John! You don't know a thing about our friendship. We don't want to be all girly." She sees Sally pulling something out of her pocket and offering it to Betty. "Oh, no! Is that a silk ribbon? Does she expect Betty to put that in her hair? I've got to stop this now." Rushing to her friend's side in the nick of time, Beth grabs the silk ribbon out of Betty's hand. "No way!" She tosses the thing back to Sally. "We don't put junk like that in our hair, Sally."

"I don't know, Beth," Betty says. "It's so soft. And it looks nice. I've got my hair in a ponytail anyway. It might look kind of cute, wrapped around it."

"Cute?" Beth is dumbstruck. "Since when did you decide to become cute?"

Sally can see that Betty would like to be more girly, but Beth is holding her back. "Look, Beth, if you don't want to look cute, then you don't have to. But Betty should be able to decide for herself if she wants to or not."

"You, shut up." Beth can't believe Sally has the nerve to say such a thing to her. "You don't understand at all. You're such a girly-girl and Betty, and I aren't that way. We like to climb trees, fish, hunt, and ride bikes. You can't look all frilly and silky if you like to do those kinds of things."

"I don't see why you can't." Sally smiles at Beth to try to make her see reason. "I also like to climb trees, fish, and ride bikes. Hunting isn't my thing, though. I think Betty can make up her own mind if she wants to try a new look or not." Sally turns her attention to the girl who's standing there, stone-still, looking back and forth at the other girls who seem to be fighting over her. "So, what would you like to do, Betty? You can tell Beth what you really want. If she's your true friend, then she'll understand."

Beth is enraged that Sally would say such a thing. "*I* am her true friend! You're just some new girl who's trying to break our friendship up!"

"Am not." Sally isn't trying to do anything of the sort. "It's just that I've seen how you run over poor Betty. She needs some help to stand up to you."

"Stand up to me?" Beth isn't someone who needs to be stood up to. She's no bully. And Betty is her very best friend; she'd never do anything to hurt her. But she's had enough. Beth looks at her friend. "Look, it's got to be me or her, Betty. I can't deal with Sally any longer. You have to pick. Whom is it going to be?"

Sally crosses her arms over her chest and waits to hear Betty's answer. "So, what are you going to do, Betty? Let Beth continue to rule you? Or hang out with me and get to be whomever you want to be?"

"I, I, don't know." Poor Betty is beside herself. "I'd like it if we all could be friends."

"No way!" Beth isn't about to spend any more time with Sally. "Me or her, Betty. This should be an easy choice for you. If you're my *real* friend."

"Of course, I'm your real friend, Beth." Betty never meant for this to happen. "We've been friends since first grade."

"Then who will it be?" Beth isn't about to give in.

Betty knows Beth well enough to know if she picks Sally, then she'll never be Beth's friend again. "I can't let Beth go, Sally. I'm really sorry. We've got history. I hope you can understand."

Sally huffs. "Yeah, sure. Sorry, it has to be this way, Betty. I liked hanging out with you."

"Me too." Betty slowly follows Beth as she walks away from Sally. "Sorry about all this."

Sally only nods and watches them walk away from her. Beth got her way; Betty won't be hanging out with Sally anymore.

Making people choose is a form of emotional manipulation. While this scene involves children, adults have been known to do this sort of thing as well.

What can you do if the person in the middle is you?

The best advice is to walk away from the situation. Betty should've done this early on in the altercation:

Beth looks at her friend. "Look, it's got to be me or her, Betty. I can't deal with Sally any longer. You have to pick. Who is it going to be?"

Sally crosses her arms over her chest and waits to hear Betty's answer. "So, what are you going to do, Betty? Let Beth continue to rule you? Or hang out with me and get to be whoever you want to be?"

Betty isn't about to become a part of this situation. "Look, I'm not taking sides here. I enjoy hanging out with both of you. If you two have a problem, then solve it. I'm not going to play the part you think I will. And you should both know that I think a true friend wouldn't ask such a thing of me." And then she walks away, without looking back, knowing that it wasn't right of Beth nor Sally to put her in the middle like that. If neither of them wants to be her friend, then so be it. They wouldn't have been real friends to her anyway if that's the case.

Another nasty trick a manipulator might play on a so-called friend is that of keeping the score where favors are concerned. Take this fictional scenario:

Bob needs to borrow a hundred bucks in the worst way. If he doesn't pay the cable bill, the cable company is going to shut him off right away. He's asked everyone he can think of, but it's the end of the month, and everyone is broke. He's got one last person to ask, but he knows the price for the favor will be astronomical – it's always been that way with Joe.

With no other choice, he finds himself at Joe's door. "Hey, Joe. How's it going today?"

"Pretty good. What have you stopping by, Bob?"

"Um, well, I wouldn't ask if I wasn't desperate. The kids will go insane if the cable gets turned off. And then I'll go insane, soon followed by my wife. So, to avoid all the insanity, do you think you could lend me a hundred bucks until I get paid on the first? I'll pay you twenty-five over the hundred if you will." Bob knows Joe will want more than what's borrowed, he always has. This time, he thinks he can put the extra part out there, instead of anything Joe might come up with.

"Oh, sure. I'll lend the money to you." Joe's more than happy to lend his old pal the money. "But I don't want you to pay me back with money. I've got something you can do for me."

Crap, Joe thinks to himself. "What would that be, Joe?"

"I need my trees trimmed. You can use my chainsaw to do it. I'll even buy the gas to run it." Joe walks out, leading Bob to the backyard. "There are ten trees back here that are so overgrown it's not even funny."

Bob can't believe his eyes when he sees just how overgrown the trees are. "Um, this is going to take quite some time to do, Joe. I'd say a few days, maybe even a week. And I'd have to do it after I get off work and, on the weekend, too."

"That'll be fine, Bob as long as it's done before the first. I'd like to have a barbeque out here for my wife's birthday, and it's on the third." He claps Bob on the back then pulls out a hundred-dollar bill. "Here you go, buddy. See you tomorrow evening to start the job."

Bob should've known better than to make a deal with Joe. It's like making a deal with the devil himself. But what choice did he have?

Bob did have choices. He could've budgeted better so he never would get behind on his bills, for one. He could've told his family that he was sorry for getting behind, but they would live without cable for a week or so until he got his paycheck and could get it turned back on. He didn't have to indenture himself just so he and his family could be entertained.

Knowing who you are asking for a favor is important. Not all people are willing to do you a favor without having you do one for them in return. And some people's favors are more than you might want to repay.

Some emotional manipulators live right in your own home. No one likes to do chores. We all have them though, and sometimes we feel under the weather and seek out help to get them done.

Jane has a massive headache, but there's laundry that has to be done. Their daughter's school uniforms are all dirty, and the laundry will have to be done for her to go to school the next morning. "Dave?" she calls out to her husband as she lies in bed, holding her head in her hands.

"Yeah, honey?" he asks as he comes into their bedroom. He sees her state and immediately knows she's going to ask him to do something that he's not going to want to do. "Oh, you're feeling bad too? Man, I'm feeling terrible today." He sits on the bed. "I've been trying to get through this day and just get to bed."

"I've got a splitting headache, babe. Tanya's uniforms are all dirty. Can you put them in the washer?"

The sigh that comes out of him is awful, "Oh, man!" He falls back on the bed. "My head's killing me too, and I feel like I might throw up. My throat hurts too. And my back aches. I think I've got the flu."

Jane just heard her husband laughing in the living room. He certainly didn't sound sick then. "Honey, you know I wouldn't ask you to do this if I felt like I could do it. Please."

"I wish I could, babe. I'm about to go take a hot shower and climb into bed myself." He rolls off the bed. "She can do her own laundry when she gets home from school today."

"She's six," Jane reminds him. "She can't even reach the top of the washing machine."

"She'll figure it out. She's a smart girl." And with that, he goes to the bathroom to shower, moaning all the while, "Man, I hope this flu doesn't last long."

Jane decides not to confront him. She doesn't have the energy to do that anyway. It's best just to do the job herself. Her husband is a pro at being sicker than she is; it's always been that way. There are other battles that are worth fighting anyway.

This one would be a losing one. He's not about to change.

That may sound like a defeated attitude Jane has, but it's more about self-preservation than anything else. There are times when we have to know certain things about people and accept them. For instance, Jane knows her husband can out-sick her. She's had throw-down fits. She's let things go, waiting for him to do what's right. Nothing has worked. He's just never going to understand her point of view. She can deal with that, or not, that's up to her. But leaving her husband over something that only happens on rare occasions seems a bit too harsh to Jane.

In life, we all will face manipulations. Some will be sneaky, some will be dirty tricks, and some will be so awful that you won't believe someone who's supposed to care about you would stoop to doing them. We all use manipulation to get what we want at times. We're all human. We're all selfish at times. And we all will be on both sides of the manipulation game in our lifetimes. It's inevitable.

Knowing how to act when you find yourself in the victim's role will help you avoid getting burnt. Knowing how these nasty tricks affect others might help you to avoid doing them yourself.

Hopefully, you're reading this to arm yourself with knowledge that will help you defeat manipulative practices. But you might be reading this to find out how you can learn more about manipulation and how to make it work for you.

Maybe you've been the victim more times than you've ever dished it out. Maybe you're seeking knowledge to help you get back at some people who've hurt you.

A little more advice – let it go. Let ugly, negative things that have happened to you, go. It's not worth it to carry around hate or resentment in your heart and soul. It festers, grows, and burrows into places you'd never think it would.

Cancer, high blood pressure, addictions, and other ailments can be blamed on stress. Stress can be caused by many things. Resentment and anger are a couple of those things. Don't let things from the past hurt you any longer than they have to. And don't let things from the past derail your future either.

Happiness is there for us all to take. It can be found in the smallest of things. A tiny yellow flower in a field of dead grass can make you smile. If you let negativity go, that is.

Manipulation is a negative device. If you want something, then be straightforward about it. That doesn't mean you'll always get what you're after. Maybe the thing you want is something the other party would rather not give – take the doing of the laundry in the scene above. Jane didn't want to do it, and neither did her husband. It's a chore after all, and who likes doing those, especially when one doesn't feel well?

Perhaps Jane could've appealed to her husband's empathetic side another way. Maybe she shouldn't have verbally asked for his help.

Let's say that she gathers the laundry and makes her way to the washroom, passing through the living room where her husband sits, watching television.

As Jane walks through the room, a sharp pain stabs inside her head. She drops the laundry basket and puts her hands on her head. "Ouch!"

Turning his attention to her, he sees his wife is in pain and jumps up. "Honey, what's wrong?"

Leaning against the bar, Jane answers, "A sharp pain just hit me. I've had this headache for an hour or so. It's not going away, getting worse even." She bends over to pick up the basket and the laundry that's spilled out of it. "I'm sure I'll be fine in a little while. I have to get this load done. It's the school uniforms, and Tanya will need at least one cleaned for tomorrow."

Her husband scoops up the basket. "Here, let me do it. You go lie down. I'm sure with a little nap. You'll start feeling better soon. I've got this under control."

Handling things in different ways makes sense. If you know that a person has a knack for something that bothers you, change how you deal with those types of situations. Not to get what you want, but to use your knowledge of how others act at times to avoid nasty tricks being played on you.

Self-preservation demands that you try your best not to get into negative situations. If you can learn to bypass as many of them as you possibly can, you'll be better off in the end.

Chapter 7 : Damaged by Dark Psychology

There have been some high-profile cases of people who've been kidnapped and brainwashed to believe in the cause of their captors. While this makes no sense to most people, the process of brainwashing can reduce a person to almost nothing. From this point, the captor rebuilds the victim, making them into the person they need for whatever reason. In other cases, the captors somehow get their victims to feel sorry for them. In turn, the victims become their captors' defenders.

In this chapter, we will look at some examples of people who have been severely damaged by brainwashing and dark psychology. There's a term – Stockholm Syndrome – which comes from a case in the early seventies when several people were taken hostage during a bank robbery in Stockholm, Sweden.

The hostages ended up defending their captors and refused to testify against them in court. Somehow, the captors had the reverse effect on these people. Instead of inciting fear and dread, they incited sympathy and empathy. Stockholm Syndrome became a term the media began using to explain how some kidnapping victims came to follow the people who not only kidnapped them but sometimes tortured them as well.

The FBI made up a data-based report, stating that about eight percent of people who have been held hostage have developed aspects of Stockholm Syndrome. Why do some people end up caring for the people who've hurt them?

Take the most famous case of Stockholm Syndrome on record – Patty Hearst. This young woman was an heiress to a publishing company. Her family, though somewhat wealthy, had no cause to keep Patty or any other family members under the protection of bodyguards. This proved unfortunate for the young college student.

At the time of her abduction, Patty lived in Berkley, California, a sophomore at the University of California, and lived with her boyfriend, Steven Weed.

The Symbionese Liberation Army - or SLA – was an urban guerilla group, but it didn't start out that way at all. This group was formed by people in a study group that was put together by a professor at the University of California, Berkley – the same college Patty attended.

This group tutored African American inmates, and through this interaction with the prisoners, the group became convinced these men were being held for political reasons more so than any criminal activities they'd been convicted for.

Donald Defreeze was an escaped prisoner who became the sole African American in the group –

now called The Symbionese Liberation Army - and the leader. Both men and women belonged to this terrorist group, and Defreeze held sexual dominion over the women in the group.

Robbing Bay Area homes gave the members what they needed. But the crime of robbery soon didn't look so bad as the group began planning the assassination of the head of the penitentiaries. They dropped that idea due to the harsh penalties of being an inmate or former one and murdering someone in that position. So, they sought out another victim. African American teacher, Marcus Foster became the new target, and he was killed by the group.

Although only about a dozen members were in the group, Defreeze touted the military strength of his group and called himself, field marshal. During this time, a woman named Patricia Soltysik began creating the group's ideology that stated they were actively against institutions that sustained capitalism. Along with those entities, they were against racism, sexism, fascism, individualism. Even being competitive and possessive were things they listed in the material they passed around that stated their beliefs.

It was the murder of Foster and the arrest of two members of the SLA that prompted the group to seek out a hostage to provide them with leverage to get their members released from prison. Patty Hearst's family had the massive Hearst publishing company with a solid reputation for being anti-communist with many political ties. Plus, Patty Hearst just happened to live near the SLA's hideout. This made her a great person to have in their possession to get what they wanted from her family who had the money and ties they needed.

Patty was only nineteen-years-old at the time of her abduction. Members of the SLA busted into her apartment where only she was home at the time. Patty was beaten until she lost consciousness. Shots from a machine gun were fired, as attested to by witnesses and the SLA claimed responsibility for the abduction of Patty Hearst. Thus, began the kidnapping and brainwashing of young, Patty Hearst.

Patty recalled being blindfolded, her hands tied, and she was put into a closet for the period of one week. During this time, she was repeatedly threatened with death by the leader, Defreeze. After a week, Patty was let out to eat meals while remaining blindfolded. After a bit, she was allowed to participate in discussions with the SLA group about their political beliefs, while still wearing the blindfold. All the while, she was still put back into the closet after the meals and discussions.

The SLA had issued a demand to Patty's family; give seventy dollars-worth of food to all Californians who were in need. This would've come at a cost of nearly four-hundred-million dollars. Patty's father did not have that much or have access to that much either. There were lots of heirs to the Hearst fortune after all.

Patty's father had to get a loan, and a couple of million dollars was all he could get on such short notice. Even though it wasn't nearly enough, he immediately got to work on getting food dispersed through a program called People in Need. This only gave food to people who lived in the Bay Area, not *all* needy people in the state of California, though. The SLA wasn't pleased, and Patty wasn't released.

All the while, Patty is still being held in the closet between meals and political discussions. But now she's given a flashlight and some literature on the SLA's political beliefs and told to read and memorize everything she's given. After a few weeks, Defreeze came to Patty, telling her his war council had come to a train of thought about her; kill her or have her join them.

With this ultimatum, Patty made the decision to urge her thoughts to be the same as her captors. It seemed like the only way to survive. She had to think like them, agree with everything they did, and she couldn't pretend either. They'd see through that and kill her on the spot.

Later, she was asked what she'd decided, and she said she wanted to join the group. Her blindfold was removed for the first time, and she could then see the people who'd kidnapped her. Her duties were given to her, and learning to use weapons was one of them. And then something terrible was told to her by another woman in the group. They practiced sexual freedom. This isn't what it sounds like at all.

Patty recounted the horrific events that followed as one of the men took her sexually by force. As if that wasn't bad enough, another man did the same to her not long after. Her will hadn't been firm after the weeks of captivity and sight deprivation. Now there was virtually no will of her own left.

Two months into the ordeal and Patty Hearst made a recording, telling the world that she'd joined the SLA and her new name was Tania. Patty became what they'd wanted her to, a terrorist just like them.

She joined in on their criminal activities, playing a part in a small robbery where she held off the manager of the store who chased after two members of her group. Patty discharging a gun to keep him at bay. Later, the three hijacked a car, abducting the man and woman in it. The man later told police he was reluctant to report the incident as Tania – really Patty Hearst - was so personable.

Patty was free to come and go as she pleased; it seemed. But she didn't go home or ask for help of any kind. And she kept participating in the group's criminal activities - even bank robberies where people were shot and wounded, even killed. If the SLA was involved, she was involved. When she was arrested, it was in an apartment with another female SLA member.

Patty's IQ had been measured before her abduction; it was one-hundred, thirty then. She was given another IQ test after she was arrested and it had dropped to one-hundred, twelve. Patty weighed only eighty-seven pounds when she was arrested. A doctor was called in to examine the young woman. Her comments on Patty were that she was like a low-effect zombie. She found traumatic injuries on Patty's body too. Gaps filled Patty's memories of when she was anyone other than Tania. It was also noticed that Patty smoked very heavily and had frequent nightmares. Some authorities saw signs of brainwashing in the young woman, while others did not.

At the trial for Patty, an expert on brainwashing was brought in. Even his expert advice didn't get Patty off the charges brought against her, and she was sentenced to seven years in prison for what she'd done. But the expert did help her in the end. He wrote an article for the newspaper, asking the president to pardon Patty Hearst as he was sure she'd been brainwashed by the SLA members. Eventually, President Bill Clinton pardoned her under his presidency in 2001.

What is so strange is that during this time, people in charge of Patty's case and her future did not believe this teenage girl could've been brainwashed by her captor. But Jim Jones, head of the Jonestown cult, was found guilty of brainwashing nine-hundred people and leading them to commit mass suicide.

Thankfully for Patty, she pretty much managed to get over all of the things that happened to her and led a pretty awesome life after being pardoned.

So, there is hope for anyone who's been damaged by dark psychology.

Let's look at a case of kidnapping that involved a fourteen-year-old girl. She wasn't brainwashed, just held captive by something stronger than chains, in her opinion.

Elizabeth Smart was taken from her home by Brian Mitchell one night. He kept moving all over the United States to avoid being caught. He took her into stores and other public places at times. There were times Elizabeth could've run for it, screamed for help, shouted out in public who she was. The whole country was aware of her kidnapping, after all.

Why didn't she ever do that?

She explained it rather well when an interviewer asked her that very question. See, her captor had made it perfectly clear that if she told a soul about him and what he was doing to her or tried to escape, then he'd kill her. But that wouldn't be enough to keep her quiet, so he added that he'd not only kill her, but he'd kill her family too.

The poor girl decided she couldn't have that on her shoulders. She could take whatever the man dished out if it meant saving her family from certain death.

What about someone who's managed to get people to do unspeakable acts of violence against others while not being kidnapped?

Charles Manson didn't kidnap anyone. But he had a dream. He'd form a family of sorts. They'd live in an underground paradise, and one day, when the time was right, they'd come out and take over the United States.

Grand dreams and less than fortunate women had Charles on a mission to collect as many women as he could. A five to one ratio of women to men was his perfect number. That way, the women could take care of each man's every desire.

The drug, LSD fueled his fire. He'd hand out the drugs to his followers then preach sermons to them. He needed to incite a war between the races to get what he wanted; to rule the United States. Helter Skelter was what he called his plan, and the group would need to commit murders to start this war. The killing of innocent people would be sure to evoke something inside of the citizens of America, and Helter Skelter would begin. Soon the country would be theirs for the taking.

Charles Manson led his followers to commit seven murders before they were caught and imprisoned.

What kind of person would kidnap a girl as young as eleven? A deranged, child molesting, rapist, that's who.

Jaycee Dugard was held captive for eighteen years by not only a man but his wife too. Phillip Garrido told the child that demon angels let him take Jaycee to help him with his sexual problems. He heard voices and told Jaycee to listen for them too.

Perhaps it was her young age that made it easier than it normally would, to mold her brain the way he wanted to. He called her Allisa and treated her as he would a wife. Not likely the kind of marriage people usually have, but a marriage of sorts. He fathered two children with her and raised them with her.

When the authorities came to check in on Phillip, as he was a registered sex offender, they finally saw Jaycee and her two children. Jaycee introduced herself as Alissa and when the authorities began asking her what she thought to be invasive questions, questions that if she answered truthfully would have her and the children taken away from Phillip, she lied.

The police thought something very strange was going on with Phillip, Alissa, and the two kids, ages eleven and fifteen. The kids looked at Phillip as if they were looking at a God. And they appeared zombie-like as well. Something wasn't right, and the police wouldn't be doing their job if they'd just left, the way Alissa was asking them to.

Jaycee wasn't a little kid anymore. She was nearly thirty-years-old. This was the only life she knew. And when she was asked later why she didn't want to cooperate with police when they found her, she told them that in order to survive, she'd adapted to the circumstances. She'd accepted her fate and dealt with it the best way she could.

And now for one of the most heinous of all of the cases of dark psychology and how it damaged a person: 1977 – Colleen Stan was kidnapped. Her captor, a married man, named Cameron Hooker, kept Colleen for seven years. His wife was aware of the kidnapping and went along with it, even participated in it.

Cameron went beyond torture, keeping Colleen in a box, much like a coffin, and hiding her in it under his bed. He kept her there for twenty-three hours a day, bringing her out for an hour to feed and torture her, sexually and other ways. This was how this woman spent much of her captivity.

A year after he'd kidnapped her, Colleen voluntarily signed herself into sex slavery to Cameron and began calling him Master. Cameron had convinced her that there was a group called The Company. This group would torture and kill her family if Colleen ever tried to leave him or told anyone what he did to her or simply went against his wishes in any way.

Once, he even took her home to see her parents where Colleen introduced Cameron as her boyfriend. She had the chance to get help, and she didn't even try to – see was that sure that Cameron could pull off the threats he'd told her.

Somehow, Cameron's wife eventually felt guilty about Colleen and helped her escape.

So many questions abound when you think about these cases. Why? How? Can there really be people in this world who would do such horrible things?

While no one likes to sit and ponder on things like this, it's important to know what's out there in the world and not to underestimate the danger that lurks.

Not that you need to live your life in a bubble to avoid being kidnapped, but you do need to be aware of things. Being aware, knowing what people can do to get into your head, that's key to getting away – if at all possible – before they burrow in and change who you are at your core.

But also knowing, understanding why some people have done the things they've done, is helpful too. Perhaps you won't judge someone so harshly if you listen to their backstory and why they did something crazy, like staying with a captor when they could've left. Or why someone committed a crime, even murder or suicide could be understood and empathized with.

In this world, we tend to see people through rose-colored lenses. We don't look for the bad in people, even though some have it lurking to the depths of their souls. This can be a gift, not to see the evil in this world and in people. But it can't help you when someone who has such terrible intentions comes into your life or the lives of your loved ones.

Learning how to see the truth inside of someone, instead of turning a blind eye, is how you can combat things of this nature. Like a bully, those who house such darkness don't stand up against people who see right through them.

Let a person, you see bad intentions in, know that you are well aware of what they've got going in inside of them and you want no part of what she or he has to offer. And if they're after someone you care about, you've got to let them know that you're not going to make it easy for them to get into your loved one's head. "You've got a fight on your hands if you mess with me or anyone I care about. Best, you get moving on, snake."

Chapter 8 : Reading People, the Right Way

Observing people might not be a thing you'd normally do. After all, you don't want people watching you, analyzing your every move and the words you speak. But sometimes we need to be able to watch a person a bit more closely than normal.

Perhaps there's a new man in the life of someone you care about. Perhaps you feel something's not quite right with this new man. You'd need to know what to look for if you were to confront him or talk to that person you care for about what you suspect is not right with the guy.

When reading a person, it's important to establish a baseline of what their normal behavior is. This won't happen if you're observing that person in an environment where they feel uncomfortable or are in the process of trying to impress someone. You will need to watch them in an environment that's neutral – say the grocery store or pumping gas.

Watch them doing everyday, ordinary things to establish what their base movements and light conversation are like. This way, you will be able to tell when they're doing something that's not in their normal behavior.

People do all sorts of things while they talk. Some use their hands a lot. Others shuffle their feet often. And still, others may scratch their heads, twist or scratch their necks or other movements.

In many cases, someone who's doing any of those movements shows that they're not being honest with whom they're talking to. But then again, some people just have that characteristic. You've got to watch the person a bit beforehand, in that neutral place, to understand if they naturally move that way or not.

Once you've got that baseline established, then you can look for any deviations in their normal behavior. Let's take a fictional scene to help understand this better:

Mike is bringing in delivery of the merchandise to a dress store he's been doing business with for a while. The owner doesn't want any items in her store that have been made in other countries. She's been adamant about this in the past.

Mike's well aware of what the owner wants. He's got a shipment of dresses that he got cheap, but they were made in another country. He's taken off the tag that said where the dresses were made and put on a tag. He had made that says, 'made in the USA.' He's confident the owner will never know he's done this, but he's still a little nervous about it.

"Hi, Mike," Sandy, the owner greets him as he comes in with the box of dresses. "How's it going today?"

"Great, really great." He puts the box on the floor. "Here you go. I've got to get going. Just sign here, and I'll be on my way."

Stacy's immediately taken aback. Mike's never in that much of a hurry, and he knows she always inspects each article of clothing before she accepts the delivery. "I'm sorry you're in such a hurry today, Mike. But I have to look at the dresses first. Surely, you can understand that."

With a heavy sigh, Mike picks up the box and puts it on the counter for Stacy. "Okay. Just try to make it quick. I've got a lot on my plate today and really need to get moving, or I'll be going until after dinner."

"I will hurry," Stacy assures him. But his actions aren't normal at all. He's tapping his foot, crossing his arms over his chest and his eyes are everywhere but on her or the box of merchandise. Stacy takes a moment to ask, "Mike, you seem agitated. Is everything okay?"

"Yeah, everything's fine. I'm just rushed today is all." He turns to look out the door. "And I think it might rain. I really need to go."

With the way Mike's acting, Stacy knows she should take a close look at each article of clothing before accepting the shipment. "Okay, Mike. I'll hurry." But she won't be rushed into accepting anything she's not comfortable with.

She pulls out the first dress and goes over it, making sure to really check it out. All seems fine, and she nods and checks that one off the list. Mike notices her acceptance and sighs with relief. "See, I told you that everything's fine."

Again, it's not like Mike to act or say things like that. So, Stacy takes out the next dress, and this time, she focuses more on the tag. "This tag just says that it's made in the USA, not who made it. What company did these dresses come from, Mike?"

"Um – uh, one here. One in the USA," he says quickly. "I guess they're new or haven't gotten in their tags yet. I don't know for sure. But I know the company is right here in the good old US of A."

Stacy isn't so sure. "Well, I'll have to know the name of the company before I take this shipment. You know my store policy. If you can get me the name of the company, I'll look them up on the internet to see what I can find out about it. I won't take anything that's not one hundred percent made in America."

"I don't have the name, Stacy. Can't you just accept this shipment and I'll get you the name later?" He looks at the door, wishing he'd never even tried to pull the wool over this lady's eyes. "You know what, I'll take the things back. You're right. I don't know enough about this company either. Sorry that I've wasted your time, Stacy."

Glad not to have to accuse Mike of anything, Stacy puts the things back into the box and pushes it toward him. "Yes, I think that's best, Mike. I would hate it if I put something in my store that I couldn't say was made where I said it was. Thanks for understanding."

"Yeah. I'll see you next week with something that's exactly what you want, Stacy. Have a nice day." Mike leaves the store, unhappy he didn't get the merchandise sold, but happy his misrepresentation didn't cost him a client.

In everyday life, we face these types of situations. It's important to be able to read people so that you don't get duped or worse. It's not always this benign. It could've been worse.

Even if you've never met a person before and have an encounter with a new person, there are some things you can look for to tell if that person is being honest or not. Maybe they're trying to hide something.

Example:

Cora is working as a cashier at a convenience store when a man comes in to pay for gas. He puts a five on the counter then hurries back out without saying a word. Cora senses that something's just not right and watches the man as he puts gas in his tank.

A little girl gets out of the car and says something to the man who now looks angry. He stops what he's doing and takes her by the hand, bringing her into the store. Cora isn't sure about anything anymore. Everything the man is doing seems a bit off.

As they come inside, Cora greets them, "Hi. Can I help you?"

The little girl looks up at the man with nervous eyes but doesn't say a word. Instead, the man answers, "Yeah, she needs to use the bathroom."

Cora points toward the back. "It's back there." She looks at the little girl who seems to be a little upset. "You okay, honey?"

"Yes," comes her short answer.

The man seems even more agitated as he leads the little girl to the bathroom. "Hurry it up."

Cora watches the man as he waits outside of the door for the little girl. He's pacing, scratching his head, cracking his knuckles, doing all sorts of movements that tell Cora something's not right at all. "So, where are you heading, sir?"

He looks up at her with narrowed eyes. "None of your damn business is where I'm headed." He knocks on the door loudly. "Hurry it up."

"I'm trying," the little girl calls out from behind the door.

Cora can't sit by and not do anything. Something's not right. So, she walks over to the man. "Who is this little girl to you?"

"None. Of. Your. Damn. Business" comes his reply.

But Cora isn't about to let it go. "I think I should make a phone call before I let you leave here with that little girl."

"What?" He tries to get past her to knock on the door again. "Come on! We need to go."

Cora decides to ask a question of the little girl who is safely locked in the bathroom. "Honey, do you want to leave with this man?"

It's dead silent as the man looks away from Cora to the door. She can feel it in the air. The tension is so thick. You could cut it with a knife as they wait for the girl's answer, "No, I don't. Please help me."

The man shoots off, heading for the door. But Cora's not about to let him leave. She's sure he's a very bad person. "I'm going to get you help, honey." Picking up a can of vegetables off the shelf, Cora hurls it at the man, catching him on the side of the head and knocking him down and out. With swift action, Cora grabs a bundle of rope off another shelf and ties the man's hands and feet before going to call the police.

In the end, she finds out the little girl had just been kidnapped by the man. Thankfully, she used her ability to read people to help save that little girl from something horrible.

It was the sheer amount of movements the man did that really tipped Cora off. No one moves around that much in a regular way. If you spot someone doing something similar, then you should keep an eye on them and how they're interacting with other people, especially if someone young or defenseless is with them. What your actions are might just save someone from a terrible fate.

You can also read someone you already know by comparing how they're acting around you and how they act around others. If there is a noticeable difference in how they act, move, talk, then there's something amiss about that person. You'll need to watch them more closely and try to figure out what's going on.

There's something called the mirror effect. This happens when you see a person, and they're smiling at you. Most times, you will smile right back, even if you don't know them. We're hardwired to reflect what we see. Someone smiles at you; you smile back. Someone frowns at you; you frown too and wonder what you did wrong.

There are things to look for in a person that will tell you if they're glad to see you or not. When you see someone you genuinely like, your face will give that away. Your eyebrows will arch as you smile, and your lips even become fuller as blood flows to them quickly. You might even tilt your head a bit. And if you take notice of the person who's brought this out in you, then you will know if they return that affection you have for them or not. Look for the same actions in their face as you've got going on. If you don't find that smile and the other things that go with it, then your face will quickly configure to look like theirs, and you will know they don't share the same affection that you do.

Another way you can read people is by figuring out who the true leader in a group is. It's not always the loudest person or even the one who seems to be in charge. The person in charge is the one with the strongest voice, the one who speaks clearly, getting to the point quickly. They hold themselves well, straight back, great posture, and often smile while delivering their message. It's this person who is truly in charge as their words are taken in by the whole group, even the leader.

You can tell a lot about a person from the way they walk too. People who shuffle about usually aren't confident in themselves. It's like they're trying not to be seen, stooping as they walk, head down, not wanting to have eye contact with anyone.

If you're in a group with a person like this or work with one, try to pull them into things by asking them easy questions. They might have awesome ideas that they're just too shy to talk about. Timid people just need a little extra attention to get the best to come out of them.

To further understand people, you should listen to the way they speak and what words they tend to use. A person who's sure of themselves will use words that mean they've thought it through and are confident with their choice. 'I've decided,' instead of 'I think.'

People who don't believe in themselves much will often ask what everyone else thinks. They then make a decision based on what the majority thinks, instead of what they think.

There's nothing wrong with being unsure of yourself. The most important thing is knowing how a person thinks of themselves so that you can understand them better. A self-assured person will use words that tell you how sure they are; I *am* doing this. I *will* do that. I *can* do that.

A person who isn't so sure about themselves will use words like; I *think* so. *Maybe.* I *hope* I can.

Knowing what kind of person you're dealing with will help you understand what they are and are not capable of doing. If you're a manager, then you need to understand this better than others do. Knowing what you can expect out of an employee is key to getting things done and running your place of business, the best way you can.

Looking for the signs that will let you know what type of personality a person has will make it easier for you to understand them. Again, if you are in management, you will want to understand your employees so that you can not only get the best out of them but make sure they're happy with their jobs and want to stick around for a very long time.

Putting all of these things together will help you read people much better than if you try to use only one or two of these things. You need to know how a person is when in a neutral place. You can't count on how they act around you to tell you who they really are. You need to see them in a group and take notice of how they interact with everyone. You need to watch their body language, and that will let you know what they really think of each person they interact with. And finally, you need to know what their core personality is, introvert or extrovert, or maybe a combination of the two.

All of these things will help you to know what kind of person you are dealing with once you know that, then you will know how to talk to them in a way that they will not only understand but listen to.

If you try to talk to an extrovert who's sure of himself the same way you'd talk to an introvert who's timid and unsure of himself, you won't get very far. That extrovert will let you know quickly and, in a hurry, that your words are falling on deaf ears.

If you speak to the introvert who's not as self-assured as some the same way you'd speak to a person you know has a can-do spirit, then you will be sorely disappointed in their reaction to your words.

Let's say that you've got a job that needs to be done ASAP. You go to Jimmy who's timid and say, "Hey, I need you to go down to the shipping and tell the delivery guy that we're not taking that order. He needs to take it back, and we won't be doing any more business with him."

This task requires a lot of backbone to take on. Jimmy doesn't feel he can say those things to anyone. "I'd rather not, if it's all the same to you, boss."

By the same token, if you ask a person who's sure of themselves to do a job that's not right for them, you will get the same response, "Josie, I need you to run out and pick up my dry cleaning then swing it by my apartment. After that, grab lunch and bring it back here. I'm going to be at the spa."

Josie isn't about to run errands for her boss. "Look, I'm not paid to be your errand girl. I've got my own job to do today."

You've got to know whom you're dealing with if you want to get things done. And if you're looking to understand who a person really is, then you must be able to read them. If you're in a situation that requires that you read a person to make a judgment call that might affect someone's life, you should know the signs that will tell you things aren't right. Follow these steps, and you'll be reading people in no time.

Chapter 9 : Kickstart to Analyzing People

In order to analyze a person, you must know the truth about them. And they're not always going to tell you the truth. As a matter of fact, researchers have uncovered just how much people lie on average.

Would you believe that over half of the people you know, and maybe even you, lie about every ten minutes or so when in a conversation?

It's true.

And within a conversation that lasts ten minutes or longer, an average of three lies will come out of one or more mouths. So, how are we to be able to really get to know a person in order to analyze them in the first place with all this lying going on?

We can learn to spot the signs people give when they're lying.

It's important to note that all lies aren't sinister. One of the reasons we lie is because we may not know something and just nod and act as we know about the subject. Even something as small as saying yes to something we really don't know about is a lie after all. That doesn't make anyone a bad person, it's just what most people do, instead of taking the time to ask what the heck the other person is talking about.

Maybe the topic just isn't something we're really interested in, in the first place. Maybe we're just nodding and going along with what the other person is saying without wanting to know more about it.

Take this fictional scenario:

Poppy is walking along the sidewalk of her hometown when she sees an old acquaintance from her high school days. It's been years since she's seen Candy and they never were friends, just schoolmates. Nonetheless, it would be rude not to say hello.

With a wave and a smile, Poppy greets the woman, "Hi, Candy. Long time, no see. How've you been doing?"

Candy is happy to see Poppy. "I've been doing great, Poppy. And you?"

"I've been doing great too," Poppy says as she averts her eyes to look at a point behind Poppy. It's not entirely true. She's been going through a divorce and life is pretty upside down at the moment. Candy doesn't need to know all that, though. "I haven't seen you in town in years. Where'd you move off to?"

Candy hasn't been doing too well since her husband passed away. She's moved her kids around a lot, trying to find work that will pay for all the bills having four kids brings. She shifts her weight to her other foot as she moves her hands around a bit. "I've been living here and there. I'm home to stay with my mother for a bit." She doesn't want to tell Poppy the real reason she's staying with her mother is because she can no longer afford to keep a roof over her kids' heads. Shaking her head as she speaks, Candy's voice isn't much more than a whisper, "Mom's been needing help for a while now. I thought I'd come home and be here for her."

"That's nice of you, putting your life on hold like that." Poppy looks at the sidewalk and wishes her parents would be there more for her and her kids with the divorce going on. They moved to Florida a couple of years ago and can't be bothered with her problems.

"Well, anything for family, right?" Candy askes with raised brows, feeling slightly guilty for not being more truthful with the woman she once had classes with. "I'm sure you'd do the same thing if your parents needed you."

Poppy isn't sure she would do the same thing. Not since her parents have been so unhelpful through her stressful time. "Yeah, sure I would." She shrugs. "It's what families do for each other."

"I guess I'll be seeing you around since I'm moving back to town. Maybe our kids will be in the same classes, just like we were." Candy smiles and nods, thinking that might be nice, some familiarity would be a welcome change for her after all these years.

But Poppy's kids won't be in any of Candy's kids' classes. She's homeschooling them. But she's gotten a lot of flak about it and some blank stares when she tells anyone about that. "Um – well, they don't go to school here. I take them one town over. It's a better school system."

Candy knows she can't afford to do that. "Well, that's too bad then. I'm sure my kids will do just fine here."

Poppy nods. "I'm sure they will. My kids just needed a bit more help, I suppose." The conversation is starting to get a bit deeper than she's comfortable with, and she shuffles her feet a bit. She's got nothing else to do but makes something up so she can move on without hurting Candy's feelings, "I've got to get going. I've got a dental appointment that I can't be late for. It was great seeing you again. Glad you're back home, Candy."

"Glad to be back. See you around, Poppy."

As you can clearly see through that scene, none of the lies told were meant to hurt anyone. None of the lies were sinister in nature. And neither party even meant to lie. They just didn't want to wear their hearts on their sleeves and delve into all the bad things that had been happening in their lives.

Sometimes it's just easier to mask the truth a bit, especially when it comes to talking to old acquaintances, coworkers, and strangers. No one wants to get into all their personal business with people they're not close to and don't trust with things they're not so proud of.

If either one of the ladies was prone to reading people and watching for the signs of lying, then she would've most definitely picked up on them. There were physical signs that both displayed when telling the white lies and even the tone of voice at times would let someone who was looking for that sort of thing know that not all was as great as told.

So that's what you should be looking for when wanting to analyze a person – even one you might think you know well. Anyone can tell you lies – even those you care about and trust. That's because we all have things we're ashamed of or just don't want to discuss with others.

You can imagine if your mother is asking you about your marriage and how it's going. You and your spouse may be having some marital problems that you'd rather not discuss with your mother -sexual problems.

Not being comfortable talking to someone about your problems is another reason that we all lie. If you can look at yourself and see what you do when you tell lies, then you're ahead of the game when it comes to watching for that in others. Not that we all do exactly the same things when lying, but the concept is the same; movements, tones of voice that change, words not coming out exactly right.

When I was a child, my mother told me she always knew when I was lying to her. I had no idea how she knew such a thing. One day, she told me her secret, "You're eyes get wide as saucers when you're lying."

Now knowing what I did to let people know I wasn't telling the truth; I went in the opposite direction and began deliberately trying to keep my eyes normal size when telling a lie. I especially lied at mealtimes. My mother wasn't the best of cooks, and she also never sat down to eat with me when I was young. So, I would choke down what I could and quietly put what was left in the trash, making sure to bury it under the other garbage.

"Honey, did you eat everything on your plate, the way I told you to?" she'd ask.

"Yes, ma'am," I'd lie, trying to make sure my eyes stayed normal.

Only I went overboard, and now my eyes would narrow when I lied. She caught onto that right away. "So, why are your eyes so little now if what you're saying is the truth?"

Drat, caught again.

When someone talks in a very high voice, who normally doesn't, you can pretty much bet they're lying. When someone clears their throat a lot while talking, seemingly giving them enough time to think up something other than the truth, you can bet they're lying. When someone looks everywhere, but at you, then you can bet they're lying.

There are lots of ways to tell if a person isn't being truthful – even if you don't really know that person. If you want to get deep enough to analyze a person, you don't always have to catch them in their lies; you just have to look past those things you deem untrue to get to the real core of the individual.

Once you know what to omit about what someone says and only count on the truths, you find in their words. Then you will be able to take that first step in the analyzation process.

Step two in this process is knowing how to read body language. Just like being able to understand the words that are coming from someone's mouth, you need to be able to read what their body is saying too.

For instance, when a person is pointing at something, there're a couple of ways to do that. You can use your pointer finger and gingerly refer to what you're talking about. Or you can point with that same finger, but this time close the rest of your hand into a fist.

The fisted point shows that you're exhibiting dominance. Think about telling someone to put something down. You want that action done quickly, and you don't want to be ignored. You are establishing dominance, and that closed fisted point is getting your point across.

Can you think about the last time you felt nervous? If you were put on the spot, you might've all of a sudden felt very itchy on your face or head. You may have even touched your face a few times or scratched your head. Your body was reacting to the nerves and sending adrenaline rushing around, making you feel the itchiness as it moved through you.

Not all body language is meant to tell you something other than what it is either. If someone has their arms folded across their chest, they might not be trying to close themselves off. They might only be trying to stay warm as they're cold.

What about a shrug? Everyone does them. Most of the time, it means a person doesn't know about what's going on or what's being asked. But sometimes it means they just don't care what's going on or being asked.

If someone comes to greet you with their arms open, palms facing outward, that means they want you to know that what they feel is genuine and they're not trying to hide anything from you.

The same goes for the shrug. If a person hunches their shoulders and puts their hands up with their palms out, then they truly don't know what's going on or what the answer is.

If the shrug is done with hands clenched into fists or otherwise hiding of the palms, then they're hiding what they know or simply don't want to get into it with you.

The showing of palms is a universal sign of submission and that you mean no harm. Authorities ask people in court to raise their right hands and recite things. This is to show the court that the person will be honest and submit the truth.

If you're being arrested, the officer will ask you to put your hands in the air. This not only lets the officer see that you have nothing in your hands, but it signals to them that you are submitting to them and no fight will be necessary. You don't wish to get into a physical altercation, and while you won't resist, that doesn't mean you're about to tell them everything.

Raised brows are a powerful means of expression. They can mean that you're happy to see someone.

You'll know that is what is meant by them if you approach someone and they raise their brows and smile at you. But raised brows can also mean that a person is surprised, fearful, or unsure. You will have to see the surrounding situation to be able to judge what that gesture means.

If you're trying out a new hairstyle and are approached by an acquaintance or friend and see them eyeing you with raised brows, you might not like what they're thinking. If there's no smile accompanying those raised brows, then it's doubtful they like the new look – no matter what comes out of their mouth.

Have you ever been talking to someone and suddenly realized that you and that person were standing the same exact way? If so, then that means you both were really into the conversation, and both of you were being honest and open, seeing each other's sides and sharing a moment.

On the other hand, if you were having a conversation and you've noticed the two of you were never mirroring the other's gestures or stance, then you weren't on the same page and probably not being completely honest with each other.

Some liars have been told many times that it's obvious they were lying as they had shifty eyes. So, you must also watch out for someone who is looking at you in the eyes constantly. This isn't normal behavior, and another way you can tell someone is lying to you.

When carrying on a conversation, most people look the other person in the eye, then look away, then look back again. It's kind of like giving the other person a few moments to privately take in what's said without the other judging or forcing anything on them. Plus, it's super uncomfortable when someone won't give you a moment without their eye contact, and most people don't want to make others uncomfortable.

While holding eye contact too long is a sign, so is standing stone still and not blinking. Most people move around at least a little while conversating. And everyone blinks. It's normal behavior. That's what you want to be on the lookout for abnormal behavior.

What about the stare from across a crowded room?

That can go one of two ways. You can feel fear, distrust, uneasiness, anger, and worry. Or you can feel aroused. It all depends on the intentions of the person who is doing the staring and why they're looking at you in the first place.

I'm sure you've seen someone doing something you didn't agree with – say being mean to a little kid. And you stared at that person until they looked up at you. You held their eyes for a moment, letting them know you have seen what they are doing, and you do not approve one little bit. Chances are, that person shut down their negative actions right away to avoid any type of confrontation with you.

What about when you saw someone who just caught your eye?

You can't seem to stop yourself from looking at them. And when they look back at you, you smile. When they returned that smile, you felt a little heat in your abdomen, and a chill ran through you. Nothing was bad about that encounter.

Onto what they do after the encounter. A cluster of gestures, in this type of situation, means the person is enamored with you. Perhaps they stroked their hair, their chin, then ran their hand down their arm while smiling at you. All those gestures were good ones in this situation.

It's pretty easy to tell when someone feels like they've achieved something. The pose is known worldwide. The arms in the air in a V-shape and a huge smile will tell everyone what that person feels like.

What about when someone is leaning back against a wall, one foot propped up behind them and sort of hanging out? You can just sense it about a person who's standing that way - they're sure of themselves and feel a certain amount of power most of the time, at least right then they do.

What do crossed legs mean to you?

Think back to any conversation you had where you had your legs crossed. How did you feel during that conversation? Were you relaxed and calm? Strong and receptive? Or perhaps you felt like you had to defend yourself a bit and were keeping things tight and not offering more information than you had to. The latter is most likely true. When people cross their legs, they're not entirely comfortable most of the time. And they will keep certain things inside, instead of revealing everything.

We've all seen the signs that someone was not only agitated but growing more and more frustrated with the conversation. A tightly clenched jaw, furrowed brows, and lips that form a thin straight line are easy signs that someone is just about done with the conversation and feels it was all for naught.

When a situation makes people feel uncomfortable, it stands to reason that they don't feel comfortable enough to vocalize this. If you're asked to do something that you not only don't want to do but have said so many times before. You feel unheard, unappreciated, and unhappy about the whole thing. You may drop your chin while your eyes roll or even dilate a bit as you're so unhappy with what's being asked of you.

What about a person who needs to get to work but misses the bus? Most likely, you will see them rub the back of their neck, clench their jaw and look up as if asking the lord above, "Why?"

Maybe you're watching a man and woman, to see if they're into each other in a romantic way. Let's say you're a private investigator who's checking out a man whose wife suspects he's cheating. You're following him, and he encounters a woman. The two talks stand close to one another, and then you see it – the sign you were looking for.

The woman says something, and smiles and the man laughs, leaning in closer. He's into her in a romantic way if he does that. And if she laughs too and leans toward him, she's into him too. Now you would know that you'd need to follow them both to get to the bottom of things.

If the two had shared a laugh, it doesn't always mean they're into each other in a romantic way.

You would have to watch how they react while laughing. If they don't lean in close, don't touch in an affectionate way, and don't end the laugh, eyeing one another, then they're just friends, and there's nothing to worry about.

Irritation and anxiety can bring about the same signs and gestures. When someone is sitting, legs crossed and their leg is going a mile a minute; you can be sure they're not feeling relaxed and calm. They may be feeling anxious, upset, aggravated, or a mixture of emotions that has their leg moving so much.

Judging how sad a person is may seem a little too intrusive. But what if you are watching a person who might be a suspect in a murder? What if they're at the funeral of their loved one and they're not displaying real sadness and angst?

How can you tell when someone is genuinely sad and upset? It's a lot easier than you might think.

Tears can be shed pretty easily by some. What isn't easy to do is make that certain gesture with your eyebrows that are brought on only by extreme sadness. While crying or at the beginning of the onset of tears, the inner corners of the eyebrows will move toward each other, instead of up. Lines will appear between them, no matter what age the person is too. It's a really sad thing even to witness, and it's real sadness that can't be faked.

This gesture can't be faked because the muscles that are used to make this facial expression move on their own, and we can't move them that way on our own. These muscles have been dubbed, reliable muscles since they can only be moved that way when there is genuine emotion that causes them to move in that very specific way.

Unless you're watching someone who's had a stroke, you can be sure that most expressions are made using both sides of our faces. If one brow is raised, then that signals that the person is questioning something said or done. If a smile is only done using half the mouth, then the person doesn't think what was said or done is funny at all.

While you're analyzing someone, it's important to look confident in your abilities. Here are some little tricks to help make yourself seem confident – even if you're not feeling it:

Hold your head up and make sure your chin is up and not dipped in or dropping. You've most likely heard the term – chin up. This means to put on an air of confidence, even if you're anything but.

While keeping your head and chin up, keep your body straight too. Stand up, tall and straight. Or if you're sitting, sit up tall and straight. Don't put your feet together while standing either. Leave space between your legs and place your feet firmly on the floor.

While speaking, use those open palms to let people know you're honest and open and that you've got the confidence to back your words up. Don't go sticking your hands into your pockets. They need to be out in the open for people to see. After all, you might be balling your hands into fists for all any outsider would know. If they can't see your hands, they can't know for sure if you're real and confident or not.

Eye contact is key, of course. Here's a two-second rule that will help you do that. Look into the person's eyes for two seconds, then at their nose for two seconds, then at their mouth for two seconds, take their face in as a whole for a couple more seconds, then it's back to the eyes. By doing this, you still retain contact with the other person's eyes, or so it seems that way to the other person anyway.

To come off as confident and to be a better speaker in general, you will want to learn how to cut certain words out of your conversations. Like, um, uh, hmm are all things that make you seem as if you're not entirely sure about what you're saying. You want to seem as if you're one hundred percent sure about what you're talking about. And even if you're not sure, you can point that out in a confident way as well, "I haven't done all the research, but what I have so far suggests that my findings are accurate. If I find out any differently, I'll be sure to let you know right away."

See, you might not know anything for sure, but it sure sounds like you do and you're ready to give new information when you get it. You're confident in what you know and don't know, and you make the listener feel that confidence as well.

When in a conversation with multiple people or even if it's just two of you, make sure to pay attention to what that other person or people have to say. This shows that you aren't self-absorbed and think you're far smarter than any of them. You must not only be a good speaker to show confidence, but you must also be a good listener.

The absolute worst things you can do with your body language is pretty easy to see. Slouching doesn't exactly incite confidence. Crossing your arms over your chest doesn't make you an inviting person as it shows that you're closing yourself off. Paying attention to your phone a lot while being a part of a meeting or a conversation isn't only annoying; it makes you look bad too. Looking away from the person who's talking is just altogether rude and makes you look bad. Being too quiet also doesn't win you any confidence points.

We all might fall into that unconfident mode from time to time. All you have to do is notice what you're doing and cut it out. Then reposition yourself and get that confidence up and running, leaving that lackluster version of you far behind.

At least for a while. Later, you can veg-out in front of the television at home where you can devote some time to just relaxing and letting yourself recoup for the next encounter when you need to shine with confidence again.

Now that you have an idea about what to look for in body language and knowing when someone is telling the truth or lying, you should know about the different types of personalities people have. After all, if you're going to evaluate someone, you need to understand their core personality.

If you've ever dealt with judges, police officers, firefighters, most anyone in the military, and a lot of teachers as well, you've seen people with the inspector personality. Sensitive introverts with great thinking and judging skills are the core of this type of personality. People with these types of personalities are into seeking insight on others, not so much letting people in on what makes them tick.

The counselor is an introvert with great intuition who thinks creatively while judging the character and personality of the person they're set on counseling to know how to talk to them in the best way. While they like to get into the heads of others, they aren't likely to let others into their heads.

While the mastermind personality isn't as shielded as the first two personalities, they are quite sure of themselves. Introverts at heart, they have tons of intuition, just knowing how many things work without needing to be taught. They think an abundant amount of time and have a knack for judging all sorts of things, from distance to amounts, and even other people.

There is a giver personality. These extroverts live to help others. They are intuitive, have great empathy for others, and can judge other people's personalities well. They know who does and does not need their help.

The idealist won't be easy to get to know. They won't talk about themselves much, especially if they don't really know and trust you. They're introverts with the ability to perceive situations and go with the flow.

Most performers won't let you into their heads as they live outside of it mostly. They're extroverts who are also great at perceiving and going with the flow. And they like to be part of the show, rather than sit back and watch what's going on.

There's the champion or hero. Extroverts with the knack to judge and perceive people and situations, they just know how to respond to make things better. But they won't let just anyone into their head.

The supervisor is great at seeing the potential in others and motivating them to be all they can be. Extroverts with a sense of just knowing who will be great at what makes them a must-have in almost every situation.

Time to get down to brass tacks. You want the fast track to analyzing people, so here it is. First things first; you've got to get yourself ready for this task.

In order to read others, you need to become a blank slate. You can't listen to another person, and all the while be thinking about how something similar happened to you once and how you handled it and wish you could've done it better. You've got to put you and what you've gone throughout of your mind if you're to focus hard enough on someone else to be able to analyze them.

Pick a neutral topic to begin your conversation. Politics, religion, the latest news stories are not neutral topics. The weather is a great one. People can always find common ground on the weather.

Take this fictional conversation:

Meg and Lane are meeting for the first time. Meg's nervous about the meeting and Lane can sense it right away. "Man, I'm sure glad that rain is over. It was a rough couple of days with all that going on."

Meg thinks about how much she loved the rainy days. "I know the rain is a real nuisance to people who have to go about their days, going in and out. But since I work from home and don't have to leave my apartment, I love rainy days. I just love the sounds of thunder and the pattering the raindrops make on my windows. I know I'm in the minority, but I'd take rainy days over sunny ones all the time."

Although Lane isn't a rainy-day kind of guy, he's glad his chosen topic has lifted Meg out of her nervous state and can already begin to see her outlook on life. Give Meg lemons, and she's likely to make lemonade.

The weather is a thing everyone is happy about agreeing on or not. There are no arguments over whether you like it hot and someone else likes it cold. We all just accept those things about others. It's one of the few things we do accept about people. All people have the right to like or dislike weather, end of subject.

So, getting on a safe topic will ease the conversation into deeper water. Water where you can get that person to dive into and hopefully let you in on who they are and what really makes them tick.

As you talk and let them talk, take a look at their entire demeanor as a whole. Don't dissect every little movement or word in the beginning. And help move the conversation in positive ways. If negative is brought up, spin it around to make it positive or put a pin in it at that time. Getting off on a negative tangent will end the conversation before it gets a chance to begin.

Ask the right questions for that person. Don't come out of the left field with questions that will leave the person perplexed why you would ever ask such a thing.

Once you've got a good back and forth going on, you can then go deeper, and as you get further into the person, you will then look for all those tell-tell signs of dishonesty, dislike, and anxiety. The more you make that person feel safe, relaxed, and comfortable telling you things as you would never repeat them to anyone, the easier it will be to understand that person and make an analysis of their true character.

Using psychology to get into a person's head is an age-old process. And as you've found out, it can be done in a positive way or a negative and dark way. But we're all susceptible to it in both forms, whether we're completely aware of that fact or not.

We're humans, and as such, we are hardwired to believe in other humans. We depend on someone to take care of us from the very beginning. Those who have access to your young and impressionable minds can wreak havoc or bring us immense peace. And most times, it's a bit of both.

Summary

Dark psychology might not be something everyone wants to understand. There are those people who are highly sensitive and can't stand to hear bad things, things that make them have awful dreams and thoughts. The things you've read aren't necessarily things others might want to hear. But if you know someone whom you believe may have been affected by dark psychology, you might want to clue them in on the things you've learned here.

People can get help and move past what has hurt them. Maybe they are with a person who is hurting them and just don't realize it. Opening their eyes to the darkness in this world and possibly in their lives is the first step to helping them.

The hardest part is seeing someone you care about being manipulated and abused by someone and refusing to see or do anything about it. You must remember that all you can do is bring light to it, you can't make anyone do anything. All you can do is try.

What if it's you who is doing the abusing and you were never aware you were doing it?

Then you too can seek help to stop this behavior. The chances are that you were influenced by someone using dark psychology on you in the past. We are all just products of how we were raised and how we've lived after all.

If you feel you've got some of these dark aspects, that doesn't mean you've always got to be that way. You can grow and change the same way anyone else can. Never let anything or anyone hold you back from making progress. Don't let anyone put you into a category and make you think you must always be in it. You have the power to change. All you have to do is see the things inside of you that you've turned a blind eye to. And you'll have to do whatever you must to change those negative aspects about yourself. Psychiatry, therapy, and psychology are your friends too, seek help if you believe you need it.

Just because we've done bad things, doesn't mean we should live our lives like we can't ever get out from under that ceiling. Many people in prison change who they are. Sure, they may still have to pay for their crimes, but the thing that's the most important is that they're different inside. They've moved on. They've grown as a human being and now know the difference between right and wrong.

The only shame is not seeking the help you know you need or helping others to do the same. If all you do is read and gain knowledge about what's affecting you or a person you care about, then you're doing something, and you're moving forward. That's what life's all about, moving forward and growing.

From the moment we are conceived, we are growing, moving forward with our lives. Time doesn't hold us still; make us stay small, helpless, hopeless. We have the freedom to grow and become anything we want to become.

The past feels heavy on most of our backs. We give it more strength than it should ever be allowed to have. Not that we can help it. We are sponges as children, taking in everything in our lives. We are molded by the people and the conditions we are surrounded by. Even in adulthood, if the conditions are right, our minds can still be bent, broken, and remolded into what someone else desires.

The good news is that it can go both ways, positive and negative. If negative has happened to mold you, change it up, and seek positively to change you once more.

We are all just souls drifting through this world. We were never meant to stay here forever. We were never meant to stay the same person we were born. If that was the case, then we'd all be drooling, whining, infants.

We all have made great changes in our lives, and we will always be able to make changes for as long as we live. If you are living in darkness or know someone who is, shed some light on things. For in the light, we all will find our own personal glory and leave the darkness far behind.

Thanks for reading,

The End